On the receiving end

തതതതതതതതതതതത

How people experience what we do in church

ROBERT COTTON and
KENNETH STEVENSON

Foreword by
DAVID STANCLIFFE

MOWBRAY

Mowbray
A Cassell imprint
Wellington House, 125 Strand, London, WC2R 0BB
215 Park Avenue South, New York, NY 10003

First published 1996

British Library Cataloguing-in-Publication Data
A catalogue record for this book is available from the British Library.

ISBN 0-264-67382-4

Typeset by Keystroke, Jacaranda Lodge, Wolverhampton
Printed in Great Britain by Biddles Ltd, Guildford and King's Lynn

എൗൠഌൠ

Contents

Foreword

What is actually going on in church Sunday by Sunday? And what do the people who – quite amazingly, when you stop to think about it – go to church in such huge numbers make of it? Where are the points at which what we do seems not just odd, but actually destructive of a sense of worship?

This book is a dialogue between two authors who are trying to get under the skin of the worshipper who is asking these questions, and in eavesdropping on their conversation we can learn a good deal about how people actually worship, and what they value from what is offered them by the Church's worship today. The dialogue form allows groups – worship committees as well as study groups – to get to grips with the issues that so often seem the carefully guarded preserve of professional liturgical archaeologists. For example, why does the exchange of the Peace provoke such strong feelings? Why, and where in the eucharist, is it appropriate to use it, and what does it do? The authors' varied experience and complementary skills enable us to enter, without the sense of being led inescapably to a single 'correct' answer, into the heart of the eucharistic mystery and to appropriate its blessings for ourselves.

The authors write with fluency and verve about the eucharist: about its relation to the historical reality it rehearses and presents, about its social implications for all those who share in its celebration, and about the promise of the life it models. This is not just another book about the origins or the history of the eucharistic action, or about how to present it. It is a more searching analysis of and reflection on what it means to offer eucharistic worship, and how that might take the Church beyond the limits of its middle-class, intensely verbal, earnest self-consciousness into the freer realms of imagination and allusion.

Why do these questions matter? It is because this celebration at the heart of our faith and practice does not seem to change people's lives in the way it should. Week by week the eucharist is celebrated, and people 'go to church' with amazing faithfulness. We rehearse the pattern of Christ's death and resurrection in the bread broken and the wine poured out, and yet we seem to expect so little to happen. Where are the signs of transformation in the life of the Church, and in the lives of individual Christians? Has Christ's one, perfect sacrifice on the cross caught us up into a pattern of life which is visibly distinct from the self-seeking, self-absorbed culture in which we find ourselves?

These are real questions, and Robert Cotton and Kenneth Stevenson will help you find answers that are well-informed, honest and perceptive. Now read on.

David Stancliffe
Bishop of Salisbury
Lent 1996

Acknowledgements

The authors and publishers are grateful for permission to print extracts from the following:

The Alternative Service Book 1980, © The Central Board of Finance of the Church of England;

Patterns for Worship: A Report by the Liturgical Commission, © 1989 The Central Board of Finance of the Church of England; Brian Wren, 'Great God, your love has called us here', © 1975, 1995 Stainer & Bell Ltd.

The passage from G. K. Chesterton on pp. 122–3 is cited from D. Barker, *Gilbert Keith Chesterton: A Biography*.

1

❦❦❦

Gathering threads

An AGM

Once upon a time there was an annual Church Meeting which ended its official business happily. After the Rector had thanked everybody – and everything – in sight, coffee was served and a general mingling of people ensued. The custom of that congregation was to invite a speaker to give a presentation on something topical in the second part of the evening.

Now it happened that this particular congregation was at a bit of a crossroads. After some years of hard slog, which had involved a lot of discussion, decision-making, and fundraising, to do with repairing and refurbishing the church buildings, people were not entirely clear about the next chapter in their collective life. Where was the Spirit leading them? What was the next flavour of Christian discipleship going to be like? On sheer impulse, the Rector invited a friend along from a neighbouring town to talk about being a Christian today. In he came, in a very unassuming style, and he spoke quietly and firmly for about half an hour. Then the questions came, first a little slowly, then getting faster and faster. Eventually the most difficult question of all was asked, namely, how to be a Christian community when the only time that we came together from all the four corners of the parish – and beyond – was in effect Sunday morning. The majority of people at this annual meeting lived in a culture in which problems got identified and addressed immediately. In fact, one could almost hear the wearisome vibes of scepticism as the visiting speaker got going. But they were glad to be disappointed. For instead of hearing a slick, well-presented, bullet-type list of easily managed targets they heard a reply – after a pregnant pause – that they would never forget: 'Hm . . . well, that's a bit difficult.'

This book is an attempt to look at some issues that face contemporary Christians, but it is emphatically *not* in the business of producing one of those slick, well-presented, bullet-type lists of easily managed targets. Not only would I regard such an aim as impossible; I would also think it an insult to the intelligence of the reader. The aim, therefore, is much more modest. It is simply to ruminate over some of the ways in which the eucharist is celebrated nowadays and the different kinds of pressure that are exerted upon it, some of them historical, some of them social, and some of them intangible. Let's take an example of each one of these.

First, the eucharist is an historical reality. This means that, even if you worship in a house church, you have to have some kind of procedure for when the Lord's Supper is celebrated. Although the various Churches of the West have been growing closer over the past thirty years in this matter, differences persist and are even sometimes cherished. So why have a service that consists of approach, Bible reading, preaching, praying, the greeting of peace, the preparation of the table, the thanksgiving, the distribution, followed by the conclusion? It happens to be the basic core that has persisted down the ages. But in an age like ours, to say 'This is how it has always been' doesn't hold water. The procedure has to stand on its own feet. History on its own is not enough.

Second, the eucharist is a social reality. This means that, even if you worship in an ancient cathedral, you have to have some kind of awareness of the other people who are present, as well as the effect that the ancient building has on the celebration. Some people will travel miles just to have such an experience. Indeed, many of our cathedrals have large congregations who gather there simply in order to escape the hustle and bustle of ordinary, local parish life! On the other hand, the old building can be so cumbersome that the congregation can feel defeated and discouraged by it. This can be the case not only with an ancient building – it can be even more daunting with a modern one. Similarly, the congregation can arrive in church on the Sunday morning with some sense of finding a spot in life where community really happens, so tight a community, in fact, that what goes on during the eucharistic celebration bears very little relation to what goes on outside. That is, unless the congregation is aware of it through its praying and loving.

Third, the eucharist is an intangible reality, a sign of the coming kingdom. This means that, even if you think you are the most conservative Christian imaginable, you are bound to change some of your perceptions of what is going on and what might go on. I remember an elderly congregation coming out of a Prayer Book service on the Sunday morning after the General Synod of the Church of England voted in favour of the ordination of women to the priesthood. As I watched them, I must confess to a feeling of slight apprehension at what they might say, for they were not the sort of people to put on an act. To my pleasant surprise I was bombarded with applause for the decision, and strong hopes expressed that this was the right way forward for the Christian Church. Here were the intangibles of modern life coming through the time-honoured words of the liturgy. For me, it was the authentic voice of living tradition, though I know and respect that others would take a harsher view.

Faith in the incarnation

History, society and the intangible, all these – and much more besides – help to produce the eucharist in any age. Indeed, one could almost say that it is the interaction of these forces that makes up the culture in which the Lord's Supper is celebrated. There is no mistaking the fact that the eucharist *is* expressed in culture-forms, just as the Son of God happened to be a Jew called Jesus who lived in Nazareth nearly two thousand years ago. And that is the most fundamental truth about the

Christian faith. There is no escape from the fact that, because Jesus is the 'enfleshment' (which is what 'incarnation' means) of God in the human race, then all that is human, our life, our capacity to believe, to hope and to love, has been changed for ever. Lancelot Andrewes (1555–1626), who was one of the greatest preachers of his age, once delivered a sermon before Queen Elizabeth I when he was Dean of Westminster in which he said: 'Christ having ordained himself a body, would work by bodily things, and having taken the nature of a man upon him, would honour the nature he had so taken.'

Our religion, therefore, is an incarnational one. It is a bold statement, a bland assumption, which lacks much meaning until it is allowed to get hold of the way we view our world. For the Christian faith is not our private possession. It is, rather, a truth which embraces us. God doesn't collapse if we can't prove something about him. He only became a human being as the outworking of his eternal purpose of love for the whole of the environment, in order to make that entire environment whole again. And he only gave us sacraments – like baptism and eucharist – because these would serve as living signs of what this new life is going to be like, a life into which we are continually washed and fed, and in which we are brought together with ourselves, with each other and with the whole created order.

All of this, of course, impinges on the Sunday-by-Sunday, week-by-week worship of the Christian community, wherever it gathers. It impinges on it not only because these are all matters of basic faith in themselves but because without this wider, eternal context, what we do around that sacred bath and that holy table lapse into nothingness, the vague introspections of the holy club. If God is God, then he is life-transforming. And that transformation must (to quote from Andrewes) 'honour the nature he had so taken'. The trouble, of course, is that when it comes to describing the context in which this 'honour-ing' happens, we are in danger of being so cool and descriptive, so detached and analytical, that we may ignore the blessings of God that lie under our very noses. How many times, I wonder, has a 'problem' in somebody's life been identified one moment only to become the 'possibility' for something beautiful and wonderful the next? There is always something hidden, even secret, about the way God works. Indeed, in a frequently ignored parable, Jesus has this to say:

> The kingdom of God is as if a man should scatter seed upon the ground, and should sleep and rise night and day, and the seed should sprout and grow, he knows not how. The earth produces of itself, first the blade, then the ear, then the full grain in the ear. But when the grain is ripe, at once he puts in the sickle, because the harvest has come.
>
> (Mark 4.26–29)

To describe contemporary issues about the eucharist, therefore, needs these cautions by way of preliminary. We cannot describe the eternal. And yet we have to say something about it, otherwise our religion would dissolve into nothingness and delusion straight away. Among the many factors that could be given here at this introductory stage, I would focus on five. And I feel bound to say that, so far from wanting to sound like some carping cleric, bleating about the way things have altered my comfortable routine life over the twenty years since ordination, these five trends are to my mind great signs of hope, seeds sprouting relentlessly and wonderfully; ours is the task to respond to the way the harvest is happening in our time. This is the way our 'nature' is being 'honoured' in this particular generation of the Christian community's onward pilgrim walk to heaven.

Five factors

First of all, whereas, twenty years ago, people still had strong denominational loyalties, they now simply go to the church they like best, and they do so often with scant regard for its tradition or allegiance. In some cases, they might even relish such a change when they move house. I have watched this process again and again. Sometimes the reasons for the change may result from the needs and interests of the younger members of a family: what is church X like with the under-fives or the over-twelves? Sometimes the reasons may result from other pressures, such as to what extent the interests of the older members are catered for at a time of liturgical change. I have come across stories of this trend all over the country. And even the Roman Catholic Church is increasingly affected by it, so that a family may be, nominally if not in law, Roman Catholic in one part of the country, and then become Anglican when they move somewhere else, where (for example) the ecumenical climate is different.

The fruit of this sort of trend is that the ecumenical movement is more manifest nowadays in the mixed nature of existing Christian communities than what we knew years ago, where congregations were much more watertight from a denominational point of view, and ecumenical activity consisted in doing certain things of a joint nature during the Week of Prayer for Christian Unity (18–25 January). I often even muse that this is God's little joke at our expense. We failed to unite in the heyday of ecumenism: now he is mixing us all up into a sort of ecclesiastical pastiche – or goulash! – for another chapter of Christian history.

That is the up-side. But there is a down-side, too: a certain rootlessness may set in. Rootlessness is often the response of a person or a group – or indeed a community – to a tradition they cannot relate to, or else the lack of one altogether. We have been told often enough that when the mass immigration from the Caribbean took place in this country in the 1950s and 1960s, people who had been Anglicans for several generations found the Church of England cold and unwelcoming, with the result that many of their descendants are now Black Pentecostalists. Tradition is not something which is written down in beautiful print. It tells how a local community lives its life. And there are many occasions when the newcomer is shunned or else not given enough space to breathe the new air of a new community. But most important of all, it is necessary for a community to have the confidence to be open to the future. Underneath many Christian communities there often lurks a particular form of religious anger. Anger is about the past, and is usually closed in on itself, perhaps a little frustrated that life is not as abundant now as it was once supposed to be. Love, on the other hand, is about the future, and is open and confident about God's power and forgiveness being able to work in its own way. Is a newcomer treated as a threat, or new pew-fodder?

Secondly, whereas, twenty years ago, people had a basic knowledge of how to get around a service book, they now increasingly need popular service booklets or service sheets which are, in the current jargon, 'user-friendly'. Indeed, producing such material has become quite a local industry among the clergy, thanks to desktop publishing. In one parish, after many years of struggling with the full, official Rite A eucharist, with its myriad options, the decision has been taken to move in this direction for every Sunday use. But it is one thing to make the decision in principle, another altogether to decide exactly what should go into it. On the other hand, it is perhaps more common to provide a separate service sheet on special occasions. Certainly the feedback from the majority of the consumers (if we may term worshippers so) is that they prefer to be given one sheet of paper at the door, rather than struggle with several items, moving rapidly from one to the other in order to find exactly where one is in the service. Such customer-care culture does not come from a narrow section of the church-going public. At a funeral party, I met a very establishment-looking London QC who regularly went to the USA. He always took the opportunity of finding a church and going to it on Sundays. 'You'd be surprised', he said, 'at how much better they are over there at assisting the worshipper through the services. I wish the churches over here were better at it.'

The result of such a liturgical scene is that the local congregation needs to keep an eye on the market in the strict sense of the term. A service booklet may provide a minimum of material, and even leave out most of what the priest alone says, for example the eucharistic prayer. I have heard all the arguments, like 'the congregation needs to learn to listen, and not be buried in a book'. Well and good. But many Christians are heirs to a reading culture that cannot be ignored by a sudden whim. A booklet perhaps needs to strike a common mean between providing everything and nothing. If it provides everything, the purpose of the exercise is lost. If, on the other hand, it provides nothing except the absolute minimum, then the chances are that the congregation will gradually hunger for more.

The down-side of such a development is easy to see and it is a theme which has been addressed by commentators, including journalists, over recent years: demystification. If services are to be 'user-friendly', then we run the risk of reducing their meaning to what we decide it is all supposed to be. In particular, we become even more captives of words than we were before. People are used to receiving photocopied pieces of paper in virtually every walk of life. When I was first ordained it was rare – a handout for a lecture and that was it. Not so nowadays. But there is more to the worship than what is on the paper. Yes, the words are important, and we shall be looking at the question of memorability later on. But the impression can easily be given that the worship of God has somehow been diminished, demeaned, by a culture that wants the meaning of everything to leap to the minds of the worshippers with immediate impact, rather like the start of *News At Ten*. It is all too easy to regard 'mystification', that wonderful sense of not quite understanding everything, as a preliminary to knowing it all full well, whereas the experience of being mystified is, at its best, the permanent life of the Christian. Do we really want to wrap up the Christian faith in such a way that it looks like a commodity bought in a supermarket?

Thirdly, in many places, the sheer range of worship is so great that local congregations deliberately opt for variety in worship to meet different contexts. It is sometimes called, in other spheres of life, segmentation of the market. I suppose that in a way it has been with us for a much longer time, given the variations within Anglicanism. I can even think of neighbouring parishes in rural Lincolnshire which were on opposite sides during the Civil War – a feature of local culture that still weighs heavily when it comes to co-operation in church life three and a half centuries later. In most cities, larger towns and suburban areas, people will travel to the church of their choice. And when a church council meets to plan some kind of new strategy, the chances are that they will take into account what other churches are doing in the particular area under discussion. For example, if a youth service is being planned, are there the resources to do it better than the big central church that can employ a full-time youth leader? On the other hand, there may well be the opportunities and the willingness to experiment with the Sunday morning eucharist in such a way that children are treated as people in their own right, not as mini-adults, and are not talked and prayed down to.

The result of this kind of segmentation of the religious market, in the end, is often that worshipping communities can become even more turned in on themselves, and they forget the secular communities of which they are a part. The position of the Church of England, for example, still means a certain readiness to be open to all residents of the parish, even if this openness is only residual, for example, in some urban areas where there are large immigrant communities which belong to other religions. But it is not just the burden (or privilege?) of an Established Church to look beyond itself into the wider community. Geography cannot be forgotten, even in a mobile society like ours. There are inevitably going to be different foci for people's lives: home, work, education, leisure, shopping. Nevertheless, part of the Christian gospel is about seeing life whole, not fragmented. It doesn't mean filling intercessions up with as many worthy causes as possible – in pressurized lives, people develop their own processes of selection, and discard information or ideas that they cannot cope with. On the other hand, part of that capacity to 'see life whole' – one might almost say, with Andrewes, 'to honour human nature' – is to give a new vision of life as it is lived now, so that, for example, town-centre congregations take notice of the Lazarus sitting at the gates without food, and the rural faithful do not despise those who have moved into the area for the first time and have to learn country ways. I admire those parishioners who resolutely stick to their local church, even when they would prefer to go somewhere else.

Fourthly, whereas, twenty years ago, church music tended to be a relatively stable area of worship, with certain recognized variations here and there, the situation is quite different today. There has been an explosion in the arts of writing both music and lyrics. No longer does the traditional hymn hold sway. Choruses and folk songs are now part and parcel of much of our worship, and reflective chants of the Taizé community kind occupy a prominent role, almost an ecumenical European culture in their own right. So important has this become that people often choose their church for the kind of music rather than what style of ceremonial (or lack of it) may be on offer. The recent report by the Archbishops' Church Music Commission, *In Tune with Heaven* (1992), highlights these trends and encourages local churches to take much more interest in the development of music, so that one particular type (whether old or new) does not hold total sway and thus isolate worshippers from what is going on around them. The result can often be that the main Sunday morning service is subjected to yet one more pressure to adapt. There are, it has to admitted, vibrant congregations which are growing with refugees from guitars! Is this another manifestation of the pluriform world with which we have to grapple? The historian in me stands by and watches, strong in the faith that the test of time is usually the best. But the pastor in me wilts a little under the force and amount of the new material, which sometimes makes all the alternatives contained in such productions as *Patterns for Worship* pale into simplicity.

Time will, indeed, be the final test, just as it has been in the past. One of the most welcome fruits of these changes has been the integration of music with the rest of the liturgy. You no longer think of saying the words of the prayers and singing the hymns. Much more is it nowadays a case of singing parts of the liturgy to old – or modern – chants. Moreover, it is interesting to observe how the relationships between the words and the music are lived out in different ways. An easy contrast can be seen in the popular hymn 'Shine, Jesus, shine!', where the words speak powerfully through the music, piercing any defences with a straightforward message. On the other hand, a Taizé chant, like 'Ubi Caritas', has a more contemplative style, where the words are not in the foreground, and the result can be a more reflective style of singing.

But there is a down-side as well, and this has to do with the collapse of a common religious culture, another result of the age of pluralism, in which many different cultures have to live together. I encountered this in a particular way when I was a curate and was planning a regional Guides' Thinking Day Service at which a special request to sing 'O Jesus, I have promised' was put forward. But what does one do at a large-scale service, attended by several hundred people, when the hymn has three tunes, each well beloved by three different constituencies? Music is always a sensitive area, not least in these big services, including festivals. There is a law in liturgical development by which worship is most resistant to change at special occasions. Who would dare to have a Christmas morning celebration without at least one well-known carol?

Fifthly, one of the major changes that I have observed across the years is to do with different types of belonging. In times past, congregations tended to be made up of an inner core of people who will go to everything, come what may, and an outer core of occasional worshippers who will roll up on the special occasions. That scene has, in many places, disappeared altogether: people go away for weekends, off-peak holidays intrude, with the result that the 'community' is a much more fragmented affair. I would guess that in many places, more people are going to church than used to be the case, but they are attending less frequently.

Churchgoing has long been affected by people's habits. In the face of these changes, it is important for the Christian community to grasp the opportunities and not sit back and sulk at them. The community is everyone, not just the regular core who may contribute far more in financial (and other) terms than others. For the real issue at stake here is identity, and how far people are prepared to give each other space to alter that identity according to their own needs and other pressures. A danger in the present climate is for the 'regulars' to see themselves as the guardians of what the faith is all about, and to look down on others. Such an attitude is really the result of an insecurity, an inability to see the truth that God is present and active in the world, and that his presence and activity is necessarily inclusive, not exclusive. So often, the parables seem to be aimed at the Christian community itself, and in this particular case the parable of the vineyard (Matthew 20.1–16) is appropriate, where the same pay is given to *all*, regardless of how long they have toiled.

But I think there is something even deeper going on as well. Identity is precious and it can change. People sometimes react in contradictory ways to times of change and crisis, even withdrawing from active Christianity for a time, or else getting yet more involved as in a haven of healing and peace. This is how people are made and it needs to be accepted, without the tightly bonded dynamic of trying to whip them back in if they have left and seem only to need to be on their own. This is the kind of open-ended, messy and inclusive community that one glimpses in the pages of the gospels around the figure of Jesus – far more so than the tight, slick, exclusive picture of the church that one can easily slip into. Identity is not a possession, it is an organic feature that is changing all the time, just as the human body is all the time changing. To affirm one's identity against others is a mark of insecurity. To live for others, by contrast, is a way of saying that I am myself, the product of my own background and culture, but I am mature in it and can cope with other people (up to a point!) without needing to look at myself all the time. In concrete terms, for many communities, that means being able to live with a mess and not worry too much about it.

Looking at the mess

It may seem a strange mixing of metaphors that when we are supposed to be gathering threads together, what we are actually doing is looking at a mess! I suppose it depends on the perspective you adopt. So far we have drawn attention to the complex character of Christian living and its relationship to worship. Some things just need to be worked at continuously – as the visiting speaker at the AGM pointed out. Then, we have to recognize that the eucharist exists within history, which means that it has to take a particular form. It is a social activity; it is susceptible to change by the people who gather to celebrate. And it is also open to intangible changes that 'just happen' as a new climate arrives, whether over words, music or drama.

More importantly, we can pinpoint shifts in church life over recent years. People do not have such strong denominational loyalties as they did. And that is no bad thing. They are less able to find their way round a set and historic service book. And that is no bad thing, either. We live in an age of increasing variation over worship, which can be expressed in drastically contrasting styles in adjacent churches in the same area. That can't be a bad thing, either. Indeed there is a lot to be said for altogether simpler styles of celebration which are themselves a unifying force in the churches. Music has become a much more important area of growth, and displays many signs of real hope for the future. Finally, people belong to the Church in many different ways, a fact that probably gives us the greatest opportunities to celebrate the human nature so lovingly taken and honoured by Christ.

It is to that nature, in all its richness and variety at his table, that we must now turn.

> Lord Jesus, our Saviour, let us now come to you:
> Our hearts are cold; Lord, warm them with your selfless love.
> Our hearts are sinful; cleanse them with your precious blood.

Our hearts are weak; strengthen them with your joyous
Spirit.
Our hearts are empty; fill them with your divine presence.
Lord Jesus, our hearts are yours; possess them always and
only for yourself.

(After St Augustine)

2

⟨⟩⟨⟩⟨⟩⟨⟩

Access to the story

Part 1

Recently a young man, Stephen, joined our congregation. He is very familiar with his Bible. He is devoted to reading and studying it, especially in small groups. He is committed to evangelism amongst his neighbours in the town where he has lived all his life. He is good with his hands and is ready to be put to use around the church. He fits in very well, but the one area of genuine unease is worship.

I visited Stephen at home after he had a chance to settle down into the congregation's way of life. He spoke of being surprised at how easy it had been to make the move from a house church to a parish in the Church of England. There was so much overlap in what he wanted to say, believe and do, even if the style was somewhat different. But in worship he found himself at sea, and resented that. The resentment was partly directed at me because he no longer was provided with the intimate and exciting times of worship that he had had in the past. The resentment was partly directed at the past – maybe a feeling that he had become too used to something that was not repeatable for ever. And there was something else, a disturbing feeling, perhaps, that he should be at home in our parish worship but wasn't.

I asked him to describe one change that he would like to see happen. He wrote to me later saying 'tradition for the sake of tradition should be abandoned'. He was well aware of the value of familiarity and traditions in worship. Interestingly, he has occupied nearly the same pew every time he has worshipped at the morning service. When his son was baptized, he was pleased to see the name entered into the registers which go back to 1908. But tradition for its own sake – tradition that does not readily show its right to be there – this 'should be abandoned'.

I couldn't let this pass unchallenged. So I invited him to point the finger at something in our worship (we use the Rite A communion service from the ASB). No sooner said than done – he pointed to the eucharistic prayer. I had guessed the answer before I had even asked the question. It was an answer I had heard many times before. Each year our young confirmation candidates are asked for their suggestions about our parish worship. Each year the answer is the same: 'Drop the long, boring bits' (also known as the eucharistic prayer). As a priest in the privileged position of reciting the eucharistic prayer, I often feel that this is the centre of such a service. The climax for most worshippers is receiving the bread and wine; but the still centre for me, around which everything else is ordered, is the eucharistic prayer. This is clearly not so for many others. The reasons why this is not so we will explore through this book.

We will start with Stephen's reaction to the eucharistic prayer. As a well-educated man familiar with his Bible, he recognizes all the words in the prayer. If he sat still for long enough, he could probably produce textual references for many of the phrases that go to make up the prayer. I can imagine that if he did this exercise, he would be left with that disturbing feeling that he also gets during worship: 'I should be enjoying this but I am not!' So what does he see in the prayer but not recognize?

- The prayer begins and ends with praise;
- God the Father is acknowledged as creator or origin of all things;
- God the Son is introduced, often as the 'Word'; his birth, death and resurrection are referred to;

- the middle section speaks in great detail of the gifts of bread and wine;
- the last section moves from the final days of Jesus' presence on earth to the final days of everything, with a brief reference to us here and now.

Nearly all these elements are present in one of Charles Wesley's great hymns, but in a way that Stephen both sees *and* recognizes.

> And can it be that I should gain
> an interest in the Saviour's blood?
> Died he for me, who caused his pain;
> for me, who him to death pursued?
> Amazing love! how can it be
> that you, my God, should die for me?
>
> What mystery here! – the immortal dies;
> who can explore his strange design?
> In vain the first-born seraph tries
> to sound the depths of love divine.
> Such mercy this! – let earth adore;
> let angel minds enquire no more.
>
> He left his Father's throne above –
> so free, so infinite his grace –
> emptied himself of all but love,
> and bled for Adam's helpless race.
> What mercy this, immense and free,
> for, O my God, it found out me!
>
> Long my imprisoned spirit lay,
> fast bound in sin and nature's night:
> your sunrise turned that night to day;
> I woke – the dungeon flamed with light.
> My chains fell off, my heart was free;
> I rose, went out to liberty!
>
> No condemnation now I dread;
> Jesus, and all in him, is mine!
> Alive in him, my living head,
> and clothed in righteousness divine,
> bold I approach the eternal throne
> and claim the crown through Christ my own.

The first sentence sets the tone that Stephen misses in the eucharistic prayer. It does so by asking the very question that needs to be answered in the affirmative: and can it be? Can it be true that the story of Jesus and his death is also a story about me? I am interested in the history of God for I am caught up in it myself. Indeed, if I know and relate the doings of God, I will better know who I am and how I fit into the doings of everything. So the first verse four times refers to 'I' or 'me' – this is going to be a story 'for me'. Therefore it is right that in the last line of this verse, Wesley addresses God as 'my God'.

The phrase 'my God' does not occur in any of the eucharistic prayers in the ASB. There are many good reasons for this, not least the fact that the prayer is spoken mainly by the priest for the congregation. Also the eucharist is supremely the worship of the whole Church, not just this parish, nor the English Church, nor the Anglican Church. So there must be a fundamental sense of the corporate and communal nature of eucharistic worship. This means in practical terms that the prayers are written with 'us' and 'our' rather than 'me' and 'my'. Therefore, some say that it is the place of private devotion, poetry and hymn writing to express a more personal and individual faith. Any desire to refer to '*my* God', they say, is merely an expression of modern, Western individualism. But is that so?

Time and time again in the Old Testament God is recorded as saying 'I shall be your God and you shall be my people'. These are words I greatly treasure. They express the deep and close connection between the story and the character of God and the people of God. To know God is to be involved with the people of God. The destiny of God is very much wrapped up in the destiny of the people of God. The nature of God is revealed within the wanderings and fortunes of the people of God. As well as this, at the time this saying was in common use, there was an intimate connection between the story and character of the people of God and any member of that community. Jews found a large part of their identity through the place each of them held within the Jewish community and the place that community held in the wider social context. Because there was this clear connection between individual and community, and community and God, the story of any one of these three also contains the story of the others. This is just what we find in the next verses of Wesley's hymn.

It is the last sentence of verse 4 that prompts me to understand the hymn as a personal one. Charles Wesley had a personal spiritual experience of being freed. For many years he had been a devoted follower of Christ but so often he had felt full of drudgery and imperfection. On 21 May 1738, lying in bed with a serious illness, he heard the words 'In the name of Jesus of Nazareth arise and believe and thou shalt be healed of all thine infirmities'. That night he found peace in Christ. He spent some of his later life caring for and preaching to condemned prisoners in Newgate prison. He saw some going to their place of execution who yet had the same peace and confidence in Christ that he had found. With later reflection Wesley combined these themes of imprisonment, death and freedom, and so could describe his own earlier years with the words 'long my imprisoned spirit lay'. This way of living was overturned by the experience of finding peace and freedom in Christ. So, beginning with the interpretation of the last sentence of verse 4, the whole hymn can be seen to be a personal cry to the God who redeemed Charles Wesley. Hence the repeated 'I' and 'me' in the first verse. But if that were all, the hymn would never have become the great favourite it is in some circles.

How does this personal hymn become such public property? First, the hymn is clearly sung with gusto by those who have had a similar spiritual experience of 'being freed'. It is not necessary, though, to have experienced the whole 'conversion' package, for, as we saw, various experiences were drawn together to produce the hymn. So some have been 'found out' by the realization of their own sinfulness ('me, who him to death pursued'); some by the overwhelming generosity of another person laying down their life ('died he for me'). Some can speak of light breaking into their lives ('the dungeon flamed with light'); and others of a sense of inner freedom ('my heart was free'). All of these are woven together with great skill. Even if only one phrase rings true for an individual, the whole story can be felt to belong to them. Wesley's words become a poetic expression of their own testimony.

Second, by using biblical words and allusions, Wesley enables us to sing doctrine found in Scripture. I did not understand the place of verse 5 when I first sang the hymn. It did not seem to belong and was an appendix to the story. The connection with verse 4 was obscure, and the sentiments expressed seemed empty. But light dawned when I found the phrase in Romans 8.1: 'there is therefore now no condemnation for those who are in Christ Jesus'. In the previous chapter of Romans, Paul writes about living under sin, being a captive and longing to be freed from a body of death. If this is interpreted to apply to an individual and how he or she feels, it clearly relates to Wesley's own story. So following Paul's line of thought the next truth to be declared, whether experienced or not, is that there is no condemnation in Christ Jesus. The hymn becomes an expression of the biblical truths in Romans, chapters 7 and 8. I sense that verse 5 is sung with gusto because it is *believed* to be true more than because it is *felt* to be true.

Third, there is the 'story of God' as expressed in verses 2 and 3. Here there is not so much direct biblical quotation as allusive reference to the biblical story. Indeed, these verses provide the context for the fourth verse. These are 'what God has done', the latter is 'the effect it had on me'. I am cautious about describing the two aspects in this way because I want to emphasize how these parts cannot be separated, and how each contains the other. Wesley made the link by including the phrase 'it found out me' in verse 3. The story of what God has done necessarily and rightly includes reference to my, and our, response.

So here are three ways that make it easy for a personal hymn to be sung and enjoyed publicly: Wesley's experience is the sort of experience others have had; there is clear reference (for some) to a well-known biblical passage; there is an interpretation of the various Christian beliefs about incarnation and atonement. I note the clear link between the first and last of these found in the phrase 'for, O my God, it found out me'. The story of God gives rise to the response of Wesley; and, conversely, the experience of Wesley directs the way the story of God is told – and so also makes sense of it.

I am concerned that the eucharistic prayers of the ASB do not make use of these three ways so as to move freely between personal experience and public expression. In practice this means that Stephen, the man from the beginning of the chapter, is left floundering. His experience is not taken up and enlarged in worship. He is puzzled, for he recognizes the words but cannot place them. He is bored because the story of God that he knows is expressed in a way that he does not know.

Before we look at what can be done to make easier the understanding and appreciation of the eucharistic prayer, let us look at one other prayer from Rite A. According to most people that I have talked to this is one of the great successes of Rite A. The prayer is:

> Father of all, we give you thanks and praise, that when we were still far off you met us in your Son and brought us home. Dying and living, he declared your love, gave us grace, and opened the gate of glory. May we who share Christ's body live his risen life; we who drink his cup bring life to others; we whom the Spirit lights give light to the world. Keep us firm in the hope you have set before us, so we and all your children shall be free, and the whole earth live to praise your name; through Christ our Lord. **Amen.**

This has become much loved by many congregations through-out the country. I know congregations that like saying it and use it as the standard end to each parish communion service. With the great emphasis in the repeated 'we' it is a clear statement of communion, fellowship together created and sustained by the presence of Christ in bread and wine. I know individuals who use it daily as private devotion, even when not associated with a communion service. The intricate patterns throughout the prayer make it suitable for slow repetition. Personally, I also use it as set in the rubric. That is, as the president of the eucharist, I declare the story of God in a way that echoes the eucharistic prayer. The end of the story is the belief and hope that the whole earth will live to praise God's name.

Already we see that it is a prayer that works on many different levels, both public and private. Indeed, it is similar both in content and form to Wesley's hymn 'And can it be'. The first sentence immediately involves us, whether as listener or speaker:

> Father of all, we give you thanks and praise, that when we were still far off you met us in your Son and brought us home.

By alluding to the parable of the Prodigal Son, the prayer describes three spiritual experiences that many Christians may identify as their own. Some will know of God's grace beginning to work in their lives even when they 'were still far off'. Some will speak of being 'met by God', coming face to face with God on one particular occasion. Whether by past experience or future hope, being 'brought home' will describe for some the state of finally living aright with God. Within one sentence the net is thrown wide and many will already feel that the prayer speaks for them, whether or not it is spoken by them. The title which the prayer uses to address God is appropriately 'Father of all'.

As with Wesley's hymn, we move now from a common expression of private experience to the story of God. In this prayer this is done in a succinct way:

> Dying and living, he declared your love, gave us grace, and opened the gate of glory.

By introducing a clear statement focused in Christ, the prayer now is finely balanced. It is not going to be merely a devotional prayer, bringing our present needs to God. There is a clear reference to an historical event which happened many years ago.

Yet once again it is not possible to tell what God has done in Christ without involving the effect it has on us. In Wesley's hymn, verses 1 and 3 end with the word 'me'. In this prayer, right in the middle of the sentence, 'us' is found. In his death and resurrection Christ declared the love of God. The end effect of his dying and living is to open the gate of glory. Sandwiched between these two phrases, and sandwiched between the cross and the end of time, we are given grace to reach the kingdom of heaven.

But the interplay between the two characters in the prayer, us and Christ, becomes even more apparent after the next move:

> May we who share Christ's body live his risen life; we who drink his cup bring life to others; we whom the Spirit lights give light to the world.

With a threefold repetition the links are strengthened between what happened then and what we need now. It is as though by looking at either character we see the outline of the other. The picture of Christ reveals our risen life and our bringing life and light to the world. Conversely, at the end of our communion and as we are dismissed, we know that the meal has not just been ours: it has been as Christ once did it; the mission to give light to the world is not ours but his also. I am reminded of the great fugues of Bach when you can hear both the theme and its inversion at the same time, each enriching the other, yet separate and distinct.

It is while meditating on such glorious things that I have to raise a slight word of warning. I find no fault in what is affirmed in any of these three phrases. The meaning and intention of the words is moving and theologically acceptable. But there is a worrying unspoken implication. That is, that Christ's risen life is only found in us, and that we who drink his cup and are lit by the Spirit are the only ones to have life and light which one can then generously pass on to others. Now, some Christians would want to affirm the truth of this, but I am not so sure. One task of being a Christian is to be so transformed by Christ's life within us that we can go out into the world able to recognize and find signs of the Spirit already there. This view, while affirming the power of Christ at work amongst and within us Christians, suggests a greater link with the world outside. This is important to say because, in practice, there will often be those on the 'outside' who are present while this prayer is said. I wonder how they relate to this part of the prayer. Having felt included by the first sentence, ironically it is just when reference to the communion is made that they are excluded. This reminds me of what one child said at the breaking of bread. On hearing the words 'Though we are many, we are one body, because we all share in one bread', he commented 'No, we don't'. This theological and literary problem of wanting to affirm the value of communion with Christ but not deny it to others will not go away.

The final sentence comes much closer to achieving a balance on this matter:

> Keep us firm in the hope you have set before us, so we and all your children shall be free, and the whole earth live to praise your name; through Christ our Lord.

Without defining who is a child of God, it affirms the freedom of us and all God's children. In Romans, chapter 8, the freedom of God's children is described, and the children are (only?) those in Christ. In a different way God can be regarded as Father of all, and so all are included here. This ambiguity is valuable, for the prayer ends, not in present experience – we cannot know now exactly who is free and who is not – but in belief and hope. In the end, we believe that the whole earth will live to praise the name of God who is Father of all.

A similar pattern has been found in both the Wesley hymn and this modern prayer. The beginning is personal, directly descriptive of spiritual experience, yet is neither individualistic nor restrictive in its scope. There is then an almost perceptible break so that the story of God is laid alongside this. Each time we noted that the breach is not total. The crux is reached when the two parts are intermingled but not dissolved into one another. Finally there is a move beyond experience into belief and hope.

Stephen will recognize this pattern. For he feels that God is active in his own life. He understands that God was active in times past, especially in Christ. He knows that the two are related and longs to find closer and closer links. Finally, he knows that although he will never experience the fullness of God now, there will always be something to hold firm to. I would like Stephen to use this pattern to recognize the movement within the eucharistic prayer. For this to work, four things have to happen:

- The words of praise need to begin directly and clearly so that a listener feels: 'it speaks for *me*'.
- The story of God needs to be told in a variety of ways that do not sound like recounting doctrine so much as retelling biblical truth. (I will expand on this in the next chapter.)
- We need more experience in recognizing allusions to biblical texts and thus making the link between life and text. This challenges the nature of biblical study in our parishes and the links with parish worship.
- We need to understand that the prayer is recited both to us and for us.

We are all involved in this, liturgist, worshipper and president.

Part 2

Sources

For I received from the Lord what I also delivered to you, that the Lord Jesus on the night he was betrayed took bread, and when he had given thanks, he broke it, and said, 'This is my body which is for you. Do this in remembrance of me.' In the same way also the cup, after supper, saying, 'This cup is the new covenant in my blood. Do this, as often as you drink it, in remembrance of me.' For as often as you eat this bread and drink this cup, you proclaim the Lord's death until he comes. (1 Corinthians 11.23–26)

At the heart of every eucharist there is the story of the Last Supper. We have just quoted the earliest account of it, written by Paul for the congregation in Corinth. I suppose that we must count ourselves lucky that he bothered to write it down; it seems only to appear because Paul was dealing with some problems surrounding the eucharistic celebrations there. People gathered in cliques, and there seems to have been some confusion about where the ordinary meal that they shared in common ended and where the special Supper of the Lord began.

It is a simple narrative, economical in words, and setting the actions of Christ within the context of a community. It is already a tradition, received by Paul from the Lord himself (perhaps with his apostleship), and now handed on to a particular community to observe properly. And ever since that time, in nearly every Christian Church, the words of Christ at the Last Supper (usually called the institution narrative as a kind of shorthand) have been part of every service for holy communion. The narrative has often been embroidered, and it has also been simplified. People soon came to expect to hear it, though they have related to it differently. Three examples will suffice.

In the Church of Scotland, which is Presbyterian, and therefore has services which are much simpler in style than those of Anglicans and Roman Catholics, the minister will read this narrative to the assembled congregation as a separate item, a warrant for the prayers and actions over the bread and wine – prayers of thanksgiving, and the action of breaking the bread. The narrative has a solemn character and it is read from the Scriptures. The congregation will listen to it with awe; the story provides them with the reason for proceeding with the communion.

In the Danish Lutheran Church, which stands roughly midway between Anglican and Methodist in ethos and style (they have a definite, formal liturgy, and they like lots of long hymns), the narrative will be recited by the pastor at the altar, with his back to the congregation, shortly before praying for the benefits of communion, and distributing the bread and wine. The function of the narrative is to invoke God's presence through his Word, hence the awesome character of the recitation – though sometimes it is sung, which sounds even more awesome. But because it is taken from Scripture, the people leap to their feet as a mark of respect.

In both those examples, the narrative comes as a separate item, standing on its own. This has tended to be the practice of Churches of the Reformation, when it was important for the Bible to hold prominence in worship, particularly as a preparation for a lengthy sermon. But the Churches of the East have always handled it differently. So my third example comes from the chapel in the Church of the Holy Sepulchre in Jerusalem, where the little community of Syrian Orthodox meet every Sunday to celebrate the eucharist in Aramaic, the language Jesus actually used. There is something profoundly moving about attending a service in a culture completely different from one's own. I went to this service on one unforgettable Sunday morning in March 1982 during a visit to the Holy Land with my father. The congregation stood in a horse-shoe formation around the walls of the chapel. The priest stood at the altar in the traditional vestments, chanting the service from a book whose pages he kept turning (for me) backwards, a reminder that, like Hebrew and other ancient languages, Aramaic starts on the right-hand side of the page and not the left!

In this ancient Liturgy of St James, which originates mainly from Jerusalem itself, the priest prayed repeatedly for the eucharist of his congregation. Deep within the lengthy thanks-giving prayer came the words of Christ at the Supper. Everyone could tell what was going on because of his actions, where he took the bread and took the cup, and raised his eyes to heaven. But around this narrative came repeated gestures which I still remember vividly. He touched lightly with both hands three things: first the bread, then the cup and, lastly, his breast. The narrative on its own was not enough. It needed to be built into a prayer, in which the intention of the eucharist was spelt out. And that intention was eloquently and beautifully expressed in those actions. For the eucharist is, first and foremost, about God blessing the bread and then wine, and *us*, the communi-cants. When I saw his simple gestures, all the long, tedious debates that have gone on in the Christian West about how Christ is present in the sacrament paled into insignificance.

It was as if those gestures were simply blowing away many of our controversies with a puff of wind.

From these three examples we can see how this narrative has been handled. Is it a warrant to proceed (the Scottish example)? Is it an invocation of God's Word through solemnly recited Scripture (the Danish Lutheran)? Or is it a story within another story, that needs its own context (the Syrian Orthodox)? I suppose like a good Anglican I have to say that it is a mixture of all three. The narrative is found in Scripture, which must be our source in the first place. The narrative has a liturgical character, as Paul himself seems to imply, by handing on a tradition received with authority. But the narrative cannot stand on its own; it needs to touch another story, the Church's way of telling its story and of why we are here, doing this in remembrance of Christ. This is probably the reason why Anglicans have always placed the narrative within a prayer, and why the new service books all over the Anglican Communion today have 'eucharistic prayers' in which the narrative is set.

Basic principles

But there are some other important principles that can be discovered in these three examples. The first is the relationships within the assembly. To read a warrant implies the need to recite and the need to give assent. To invoke God's Word on his people implies the need to state the character of God's grace, God's indwelling power among his people. To recite the narrative within a longer prayer implies that the community has its own version of the wider story of why it is there in the first place. In other words, there is a relationship between the present and the past, expressed in the role of the minister, pastor, priest, or president with the rest of the congregation. In fact, it is not just the past and the present; it also includes the future, since the eucharist, though existing within time, is timeless: 'For as often as you eat this bread and drink this cup, you proclaim the Lord's death *until he comes*' (1 Corinthians 11.26).

All this means that the eucharist is by its nature relational, and it needs conventions by which the relationship between president and community is inaugurated and expressed, starting with the traditional dialogue:

> The Lord be with you. **And also with you.**
> Lift up your hearts. **We lift them to the Lord**.
> Let us give thanks to the Lord our God. **It is right
> to give him thanks and praise**.

Another way of expressing this relationship is to break the eucharistic prayer up into sections, punctuated with responses by the rest of the congregation. This is by no means a new feature – the various Eastern Churches have known the practice for centuries. We have become accustomed to 'Christ has died, Christ is risen, Christ will come again', and a recent composition by the Liturgical Commission of the Church of England includes the option to repeat 'To you be glory and praise for ever' at certain stages throughout the prayer. The difficulty with such responses is that if they are too frequent and always changing, the congregation can get lost in the service booklet, a criticism that has been voiced with some justification recently.

But there are two further principles that arise from the examples given earlier. One is to do with the question of variety. Why have alternative eucharistic prayers? In the Church of Scotland, the narrative remains the same, but the prayer of thanksgiving afterwards may well change, and has changed across the years. Similarly, in the Lutheran example, the narrative obviously remains static, but the prayers which follow have altered. In the Syrian Orthodox Church, other eucharistic prayers may be used. Indeed, there was a time when no fewer than seventy was the extent of the possible repertoire! After the Second Vatican Council, much discussion in the Roman Catholic Church centred on what to do with the old eucharistic prayer that dated back to early times. Eventually, after advice, Pope Paul VI took the decision to restore it to its early form, but to have three additional eucharistic prayers composed, which would draw on older sources which had been ignored for centuries. This is why the 1970 Missal has these alternative prayers. And other Churches followed suit.

Variety in telling the story is a fine thing in principle. But it can destabilize the congregation and give the impression that those who preside are simply indulging themselves. Where alternative prayers are used, it is important to have a basic core, a basic shape to the prayer, so that congregations know roughly when items are going to come. This has been achieved in the Alternative Service Book, though the extent of real variation is perhaps not as great as it might be; which is why its revision in the year 2000 is going to be an interesting process.

But a much more profound principle can easily be forgotten. It has to do with participation itself. For centuries, the eucharistic prayer was in many places recited silently. People nowadays find this beyond comprehension. But there must have been a reason for this move in the first place, and I suspect it was to do with the sense of the holy in our midst. A whispered voice can be a very eloquent one, especially in a building resonant with rich acoustic. I am not arguing for its reintroduction, but I am suggesting that one does not have to recite something in order to participate. To make a prayer one's own is a much more subtle business. It is to do with knowing the prayer, loving and cherishing it, and seeing new riches within it as these unfold.

Horizontal and vertical

The eucharist is about fellowship with God and with each other. One of the ways in which this has been expressed is to talk about a horizontal fellowship and a vertical one. Put at its simplest, the way in which the Lord's Supper is celebrated can bring this across in ways that make words seem secondary. A church with an altar at the east end and a priest standing with his or her back to the congregation is one way of saying that the eucharist implies a vertical fellowship, with all the pointing in the direction of the transcendent that surrounds such an arrangement. By contrast, a church with a centrally positioned table round which the community gathers is a way of saying that the eucharist is about horizontal fellowship, a God who is 'immanent', resting within human life.

Of course, the eucharist is about both, and it would be a foolish age that espouses one style and approach at the expense of another. What is going on at present is a kind of see-saw; when I was a small boy, communion was carefully prepared for, individualist in style, and one approached the altar with a strong sense of meeting the high and mighty Lord. Nowadays, the kind of piety is quite different. Communion is not so carefully prepared for, and one goes along to church to rejoice with the fellowship of other people, with much singing and praise. Perhaps a balance is needed; alongside all the jolly Lord's Suppers that are on offer mid-morning, I hope that the quiet, contemplative ones at an earlier (or a later) hour remain. We need all temperaments in the Church.

The vertical–horizontal balance is also encountered in the words of the eucharistic prayer. To what extent should it vary according to the occasion and to what extent should it be fixed? Obviously a careful balance is needed here, as well. One way to achieve this is to include proper insertions into the prayer. These can vary according to the season or the pastoral occasion. I once took a confirmation class through the Proper Prefaces in the back of the Rite A Eucharist book and asked them which ones they preferred at the particular seasons, and why. It was interesting to see how, when it came to Easter, each one of them opted for the cosmic-pastoral language of this particular example:

> And now we give you thanks because in his victory over the grave a new age has dawned, the long reign of sin is ended, a broken world is being renewed, and the human race is once again made whole.

Time is central, for within its bounds we live and move and have our being. In words that remind me of watching a ship go by at night, Augustine describes the passage of time in the tenth Book of his *Confessions*: 'Time must come out of the future, pass by the present, and go into the past: so it comes from what as yet does not exist, passes through that which lacks extension, and goes into that which is now non-existent.' In other words, time affects the eucharist, and that includes not only where we stand in relation to ourselves (getting married, attending a baptism, or a funeral), but also where we are in relation to the rest of the world, which is why the church year is so central. Anniversaries give richness and context to what can otherwise seem a bald and egocentric existence! Anniversaries, whether of Christ's birth, death, resurrection, ascension, transfiguration – or whatever – provide the opportunity to focus on one particular truth in the Christian gospel. For narrative – in the widest sense of the term – helps to form a community. The Jewish Passover continues to feed millions of people all over the world by its simple power to recall an event that shaped a community for ever. So with the eucharist: it is full of unsearchable riches whereby Christians are enabled to live again the life of faith, in that creative tension, that paradox, that mystery, which is bound up with a God who is both high and mighty and deeply embedded within us.

Other dimensions

Part of the genius of the eucharistic prayer, part of its elusive accessibility, is that there are always new dimensions to its life and power. Not all eucharistic prayers are great works of art, and I have heard a few that I would gladly consign to the wastepaper basket! I have also come across occasions when, in the interests of egalitarianism, the whole congregation recited the institution narrative, and it sounded ghastly, at least to my ears. Furthermore, one of the weaknesses of many modern prayers results from the undue speed with which these prayers were composed. It takes time to create, and to create eloquently. (And by eloquence I do not necessarily mean long-windedness, though many modern prayers, for example the collects, have been justly criticized for being too short, too ready to be finished too soon.) But there are a number of dimensions to the prayer that deserve pondering.

One is the way in which the heavenly and the earthly meet. It is not a fashionable notion in some circles, and I think this is partly because we have gone too far down the road of the 'horizontal' approach to the eucharist. I suppose it focuses on two points in the prayer. One is the Sanctus ('Holy, holy, holy'), where the union of heaven and earth is made explicit. No one knows exactly when this Jewish hymn was incorporated into the eucharistic prayer, but we think that it happened quite early, perhaps in the late third century. Why? Not in the interests of Jewish–Christian relations – not then! But, I suspect, because it became increasingly necessary to give the Christian eucharist a sense of being more than the sum total of those attending a particular service in a particular place. To join with the worship of heaven is to say something reciprocal about what we are doing: we join with heaven, heaven joins with us. The other focus comes when, as is sometimes the case, the saints are mentioned in the prayer; and I wish that more prayers would restore this.

The third eucharistic prayer in the Alternative Service Book expresses this somewhat fitfully:

> Send the Holy Spirit on your people and gather into one in your kingdom all who share this one bread and one cup, so that we, in the company of all the saints, may praise and glorify you for ever . . .

The Book of Common Prayer (1979) of the Episcopal Church of the USA goes even further:

> Unite us to your Son in his sacrifice, that we may be acceptable through him, being sanctified by the Holy Spirit. In the fullness of time, put all things in subjection under your Christ, and bring us to that heavenly country where, with all your saints, we may enter the everlasting heritage of your sons and daughters.

Then there is the question of imagery. We need richer imagery – and we are slowly getting there. Sometimes images can be partly biblical and partly those used and adapted by Christian writers across the centuries. One of the finest examples of these is to be found towards the end of the second eucharistic prayer in the Alternative Service Book:

Accept through him this offering of our duty and service; and as we eat and drink these holy gifts in the presence of your divine majesty, fill us with your grace and heavenly blessing; nourish us with the body and blood of your Son, that we may grow into his likeness and, made one by your Spirit, become a living temple to your glory.

The movement of the prayer at this point is unmistakable; Christ is the centre, and the communicants are gathered into the presence of God, to be filled with his power, and to grow into the likeness of Christ by the Holy Spirit. Human nature is transformed.

With the question of imagery comes also the kind of words we must expect the liturgy to use. At root, the kind of words that enrich prayer is the language of *showing*, rather than *saying*. Words that resonate and point beyond themselves, and which cluster together to form a rich whole are more likely to help worshippers than words which define and sound contrived, and which hit other words with meaning and fight for their own life. I think, too, that we, who live in a culture where words have great power but can so often sound meaningless because we do not always trust them, need to learn to relate to the language of prayer in a different way. And we need to listen to what poets are saying about religious experience, too. We have not yet arrived at a stage at which we can confidently say that a new form of liturgical English has been brought to birth. We have to keep working at it. And nowhere is this clearer than in the great prayer of the Church around the Lord's table, the eucharistic prayer.

A sense of wonder

I remember once taking a group of children into an old church. Many of them had never been inside one before and it was breathtaking to enjoy their amazement. They stood and gazed and gazed, looking upward and around and into this and that nook and cranny. In short, they loved every moment.

I am not making a plea for leaving our brains and analytical equipment outside the church building every time we come to the eucharist. But I am suggesting that there is much more to the human soul before God than those important God-given capacities, capacities which are so important for the modern world to function at all properly. But we do need to recapture a sense of wonder, not for its own sake, but because it will help to set in a right perspective our own relationships, with each other, our planet and ourselves. Many Christian writers have identified the 'tree of life, which is in the paradise of God' (Revelation 2.7) with the eucharist. One of the greatest mystics of the seventeenth century, Thomas Traherne, reflects thus on the wonder of God's redemptive work in creation:

> Would men consider what God hath done, they would be ravished in spirit with the glory of His doings. For Heaven and Earth are full of the majesty of His glory. And how happy would men be could they see and enjoy it! But above all these our Saviour's cross is the throne of delights. That Centre of Eternity, that Tree of Life in the midst of the Paradise of God!

3

Access to forgiveness

Part 1

A teacher at our school told this story. She was dreaming that she was playing the cello in a performance of Handel's *Messiah*. Suddenly she woke up to find that she was playing the cello in a performance of Handel's *Messiah*! Even as I heard the story for the first time it sounded apocryphal. But that made it even better – the story is 'true' for hundreds of performers. Many people can sing, play and hum the *Messiah* even in their sleep. For many, a yearly performance is part of their culture and tradition. The reasons for this must begin with the superb and joyous nature of much of the music. Also the libretto is so popular. Often when I ask for people's favourite Bible verses I find that the answers are included in the words of the *Messiah*. But there is something more: the 'story' of the *Messiah* is a story they recognize. The collection of texts that forms the libretto is, from the point of view of biblical scholarship, amazingly haphazard. Yet it gives expression to the story of God that many find deeply satisfying and true to life.

So here is an account of what we find in Handel's *Messiah* with 'continuity' provided between the various texts. The title of the arias referred to are placed in brackets.

The story does not begin 'in the beginning'. It begins abruptly. Immediately we realize that much of significance has already happened, but no reference is made to this. The best way I can think of describing this is 'on awakening we find ourselves in a foreign land'. When we recognize where we are, we realize we are out of keeping with our surroundings. The gods and tradition of this land are not our own ('For behold, darkness shall cover the earth' and 'The people that walked in darkness'). This gives rise to our feeling confused, lost and fearful – but not abandoned. For the command of God comes to us to speak comfort to our people ('Comfort ye my people'), to tell them that all shall be well. God is going to reveal his glory ('And the glory of the Lord') by gathering together all those who have been scattered abroad. We need to be made ready for this ('And he shall purify'), for God's coming to us will be seen by everyone ('O thou that tellest good tidings to Zion'). God comes in the form of the Prince of Peace ('For unto us a child is born'). It is Jesus who does the things we expect of God: feeding the hungry, bearing up the weary ('He shall feed his flock') and showing the way to those who are lost ('Then shall the eyes of the blind'). God gathers together his people, then leads them back home.

That in essence is the story, but it needs to be filled out some more. Parts 2 and 3 of the *Messiah* describe the cost and the result of the story. Just as no reason is given for the story beginning 'in a foreign land', so no explanation is given of why there is evil. But there is wickedness and law breaking ('Surely he hath borne our griefs'), and for the end to be reached these need to be overcome ('Behold the Lamb of God'). Some of the wrongdoing is ours ('All we like sheep have gone astray'), some is direct opposition by others ('Why do the nations so furiously rage together') to the force of good. For Jesus to be the gatherer and leader, he comes amongst us and joins in the pain of our situation ('And with his stripes we are healed'). But his lot is not to be left there ('He trusted in God'), he is not abandoned ('But thou didst not leave his soul in hell'), and so we are not abandoned either.

The result is the establishment of God's kingdom ('Hallelujah'). The old country was the place of death and destruction ('Since by man came death'). The new kingdom is the place of resurrection ('The trumpet shall sound') and victory ('But thanks be to God'). We have been brought back to God by Christ ('Worthy is the Lamb that was slain') and here we shall meet with God ('I know that my redeemer liveth'). The victory is God's now and for ever.

One aspect of this story that may strike you is the difficulty of beginning it. The first aria, 'Comfort my people', takes us into a situation where so much has already happened. The pull of the music and words is forward: speak comfort to my people and tell them that *this* is over. But some attention needs to be backward-looking to describe what *this* refers to. Why do we need comfort? What do we need to be delivered from? Where are we?

This, of course, matches the surprise anyone may have on reading the book of the prophet Isaiah. Suddenly at the end of chapter 39 there is a break. So much must have happened between then and what is recorded in chapter 40. But of this there is no record. I deeply regret this, for I find the story of the return from exile moving and satisfying. But also I value the silence, for it makes the beginning not only more startling but also more open to interpretation. We will return to this later.

I now want to turn to another 'story' that is found in the Bible and used frequently in worship and liturgy. This is the story of the Exodus. This is much more familiar, as not only is the story recorded in graphic and interesting detail throughout the book of Exodus but also it is so frequently used again in the New Testament. Many different parts of the story are put to use to explain and interpret the meaning of who Jesus was and what he did.

Both stories are a narrative of a journey. Both stories have God as the lead character and God's people fulfilling the subordinate role. Yet there are major differences between the stories. I want to identify some of these and so distinguish two types. By doing this, I want also to encourage the use of other stories as a pattern for use in prayer and worship. The familiarity of the Exodus pattern has tended to overwhelm the other patterns. This is a shame because some people will naturally recognize their personal story in the Exile pattern. If this is then read in liturgy, there is a far greater chance that the liturgy will feel familiar and expressive of their experience of God.

In the Old Testament reading set in the Book of Common Prayer for the Sunday next before Advent, there is a verse that justifies my endeavour to distinguish these stories. It reads:

> Therefore the time is coming, says the Lord, when people will no longer swear 'by the life of the Lord who brought the Israelites up from Egypt'; instead they will swear 'by the life of the Lord who brought the descendants of the Israelites back from a northern land and from the lands to which he had dispersed them'; and they will live on their own soil.

The prophet is encouraging the people of God to review their vision of God. God is not only, not merely, the One who brought the Israelites up from Egypt, but he is the One who could bring them back out of exile. The former title need not be abandoned. Rather, God must not be limited to that description alone; and so the way God works with us is not to be limited to the pattern of the Exodus alone.

Let us now turn our attention briefly to the Exodus story. We will do so once again, but not by looking straight at the biblical text. Rather, we will see how this has been interpreted in a liturgical form: the prayer of blessing used at the font over the water of baptism. I find this a beautiful prayer to say because it is clear and easy to phrase. It has a dynamic structure and a flow. It can properly be seen as the central proclamation of the story of God's saving love in the service of baptism. For our purpose the clarity of this prayer makes it easy for us to recognize the pattern of the story.

> Almighty God, whose Son Jesus Christ
>   was baptised in the river Jordan;
> we thank you for the gift of water
>   to cleanse us and revive us;
> we thank you that through the waters of the
>   Red sea, you led your people out of slavery
>   to freedom in the promised land;
> we thank you that through the deep waters
>   of death you brought your Son, and raised
>   him to life in triumph.

Bless this water, that your servants who are
washed in it may be made one with Christ
in his death and in his resurrection,
to be cleansed and delivered from all sin.
Send your Holy Spirit upon them to bring
them to new birth in the family of your
Church, and raise them with Christ to full
and eternal life.
For all might, majesty, authority, and power
are yours, now and for ever.

There are three strands in the prayer: the Exodus story, the life of Jesus, and baptism today. The prayer achieves its depth and resonance by laying these strands alongside each other, and by drawing out the parallels between the strands. At the beginning of the prayer, a reminder of Jesus' baptism places in context this gift of water. The key word 'thank' then links us both to the Exodus and back to the life of Jesus. The journey of the Exodus is related as one from slavery to freedom. The passage is through the Red Sea; the goal is the Promised Land. Then the Pauline interpretation, familiar to us from Romans, chapter 6, is placed upon the story. Our journey is from sin and death to life by being made one with Christ. We enter into a new life thanks to the power and might of God.

The pattern of this story can be contrasted with the story of the Exile. In both we find similar components:

- the action of God that is decisive for human salvation and sufficient in itself: either in God as the true leader of his people (Exile) or in Christ's victory on the cross and resurrection (Exodus);
- a portrayal of human need: in both cases the people of God begin in a foreign land with a life that is imperfect and needs reviving;
- a triumphant resolution: enemies are defeated or destroyed (Exodus) or the journey back home is completed in safety (Exile).

But these are described in different, subtle ways. Moreover, the order in which they are held together is not equivalent. There is a *theological order*: by this I mean that the work of God must be seen as primary, more important and more fundamental than an explanation of human need. There is also a (possibly different) *order of spiritual experience*: we may come to understand and appreciate our need before we know how that need is to be met. I have frequently heard confusion about these orders in evangelistic services. Typically, a man presents his testimony wanting to convey the marvellous nature of conversion but spends more time and energy on a vivid description of his sinful past than on the work of God bringing him to salvation. The presentation seeks to win our attention by its description of vice and greed so that we will also be ready to listen to the 'religious' part, explaining about God. This is a dangerous pattern to follow: the first half of the story is likely to be much more interesting! Anyway, it seems to imply that we cannot hear the message of God without first passing through a stage of focusing on our human need. The pattern of the story actually provides an unnecessary barrier to the experience of salvation.

The same pattern can be found in preaching. An evangelistic service may begin with a moving account of God's total acceptance of us. The heart of the gospel is portrayed in God's overwhelming love freely available to us just as we are. The preacher will draw on examples of Jesus associating with tax-gatherers and sinners to generate a deep sense of God's welcoming love. Then the sermon may stutter slightly, and the perceptive listener will hear the preacher backtracking. Although this is true, he may say, to make it your own you have first to admit your need for God. Note the 'first'. It is as though the preacher has told you about crossing the Red Sea and offered you a glimpse of the promised land, but first you are required to take yourself into Egypt. This requirement is theologically unnecessary. We do not have to take ourselves there. That is where we find ourselves; or better, that is where we are found.

The story of the Exile gives voice to this. It begins with a sense of being found by God. We recognize that life is not as it should be, that we are out of relationship with ourselves, our neighbours, our world, that we are in a 'foreign land'. This recognition originates in the call from God to move on and leave. At the beginning there need be no sense of guilt or shame; we need not yet consider who has responsibility for the estrangement we feel. The essential matter is that all begins with God's word of comfort, declaring that 'our warfare is ended, our iniquity is pardoned' (Isaiah 40.2). Here is the marvellous paradox, that we can begin with forgiveness before confession. In the anecdote that began this chapter the teacher woke up to find herself living the reality of her dream. In a similar way, we can be woken up by God's grace to find that we are already involved in the story of redemption and forgiveness. Our confession is not an entry requirement to that story, for God has already begun his healing work in us.

The Exile story is about a journey back home. Rather than a journey to a new, unknown promised land (Exodus), we are being brought back to what is familiar. This makes sense to those whose spiritual experience of God is not one of conversion, leaving Egypt behind and entering upon a new lifestyle, but one of being led deeper into a fuller engagement with what is already known. God is portrayed as the one who unifies rather than separates out. 'The Lord is rebuilding Jerusalem, he is gathering together the scattered outcasts of Israel' (Psalm 147.2). Throughout the chapters of Isaiah 40 to 55 God is described as gathering gently, leading his people young and old in one body through the desert. This contrasts with the powerful destruction of enemies at the Exodus. Indeed, the thrust of the story is to include rather than exclude, and God's intention is that salvation 'may reach to the end of the earth' (Isaiah 49.6).

This story is not an unrealistic idealization of life, for these chapters are shot through with the figure of the Lord's Servant (Isaiah 42.1–4; 49.1–6; 50.4–9; 52.13 – 53.12). God may be the initiator and prime mover of the story, but the Servant accomplishes God's will. It is in this figure of the Servant that we see suffering, rejection and oppression accepted and borne for us.

The power of this story lies in the simplicity of its language. 'All we like sheep have gone astray; we have all turned to our own way, and the Lord has laid on him the iniquity of us all' (Isaiah 53.6). Here we read a plain description of our human nature – we all do go astray – with no requirement for us to do anything, because God is the one who has already done what is required, laid our iniquity on the Servant.

It is important to distinguish these two stories because, though they carry much of the same theological content, they are able to affirm different spiritual experiences. Those who have been baptized as infants may have a deep sense of always being with God. From earliest days as well as in each present day, they can have a sense of God being in the midst of life offering them comfort and calling them to proclaim comfort to others. This is why the opening aria of the *Messiah* is such a moving moment. Also, the pattern of this story is repeatable, for it is essentially about returning home and finding life with God where I already am. So personally I do not find it difficult to understand having a number of 'conversion' experiences in this pattern. Each time in a different way I am being found by God and led back into greater wholeness. I therefore understand my own baptism as the once-and-for-all joining of the people of God, though I may need to return from exile throughout my life. In contrast to this, the Exodus story cannot easily interpret repeated conversions. Those who have lost a feel of the new-ness of their promised land may be tempted to repeat the unrepeatable journey of baptism into Christ. Far better is for them to find in the Exile story a new and fresh understanding of God bringing them home.

My hope is that this pattern will become represented in liturgical texts more frequently. For then more worshippers will identify with or recognize that the liturgy speaks for them and to them. One example that has occurred in a recent prayer is the phrase 'when we were still far off, you met us in your Son and brought us home'. This could be effectively used in a baptismal as well as a eucharistic prayer. One ancient text with similarities to the Exile pattern that is already used by many each day is the Benedictus, the Canticle from Luke's gospel traditionally recited each day at Morning Prayer.

> Blessed be the Lord the God of Israel:
> for he has come to his people and set them free.
>
> He has raised up for us a mighty saviour:
> born of the house of his servant David.
>
> Through his holy prophets he promised of old:
> that he would save us from our enemies,
> from the hands of all that hate us.
>
> He promised to show mercy to our fathers,
> and to remember his holy covenant.
>
> This was the oath he swore to our father Abraham:
> to set us free from the hands of our enemies,
>
> free to worship him without fear:
> holy and righteous in his sight all the days of our life.
>
> You my child shall be called the prophet of the Most High:
> for you will go before the Lord to prepare his way,
>
> to give his people knowledge of salvation:
> by the forgiveness of all their sins.
>
> In the tender compassion of our God:
> the dawn from on high shall break upon us,
>
> to shine on those who dwell in darkness and the shadow of
>   death:
> and to guide our feet into the way of peace.

I see the similarities in its beginning with God's initiative not our need, and the description of God as the one who creates the setting for our life, drawing us away from our enemies. There is explicit reference to the Exile by John the Baptist (the child) being called the one who will prepare the way of the Lord (Isaiah 40.3). As we use this prayer now, we acknowledge that this way has to be prepared in our own day.

The Benedictus also describes at its centre the nature of what we are being freed for: to be holy and righteous. The use of these words belongs in the Greek world where to be righteous meant to live in moral harmony with other human beings and to be holy meant to pay one's dues to God. As we are drawn closer to God we are called both into fuller righteousness and into deeper holiness. That calling changes us. As we are changed we learn to forgive and experience forgiveness. This properly combines the forgiving and the being forgiven just as the Lord's Prayer does. There is continuity between the saving act of God at the beginning and the result of this act as shown in our lives.

Part 2

Baptism an imperative

Right at the end of Matthew's gospel, Jesus has this to say to his disciples:

> All authority in heaven and on earth has been given to me. Go therefore and make disciples of all nations, baptising them in the name of the Father and of the Son and of the Holy Spirit, teaching them to observe all that I have commanded you; and lo, I am with you always, to the close of the age. (Matthew 28.18–20)

Here are the last recorded words of Jesus in the first book of the New Testament. Brushing aside questions of origin and authenticity, we may observe that Jesus does a number of things. He claims authority; he tells his disciples to preach in all the world; and they are to baptize in the threefold name of the Trinity (the earliest occurrence of the Trinity in the New Testament); and they are to keep Christ's commandments. Jesus' words end with the telling promise of his presence until the end of time.

We get an even wider picture if we compare this passage with two others from the same gospel. Right at the beginning, when Joseph discovers that Mary is pregnant and is on the point of doing exactly what is within his rights, namely to divorce her from the contract of betrothal because she was with someone else's child (in those days, betrothal was legally binding), he has a dream in which he is told the truth about Jesus. And the story continues: 'All this took place to fulfil what the Lord had spoken by the prophet: "Behold, a virgin shall conceive and bear a son, and his name shall be called Emmanuel" (which means, God with us)' (Matthew 1.22–23). In other words, Jesus' birth is 'God with us'. If we take that theme with the last words he says – 'I am with you always' – we are struck by an important Christian truth: the abiding presence of God in our midst.

The other passage with which to compare Jesus' parting words is to be found in the narrative of the baptism of Jesus:

> And when Jesus was baptised, he went up immediately from the water, and behold, the heavens were opened and he saw the spirit of God descending like a dove, and alighting on him; and lo, a voice from heaven, saying, 'This is my beloved Son, with whom I am well pleased.' Then Jesus was led up by the Spirit into the wilderness to be tempted by the devil. (Matthew 3.16 – 4.1)

Jesus is not only God's presence among us. He also shares our human nature, which includes the need to be baptized along with John's other followers, *and* the tough experience of being tempted in the wilderness. The importance of this cannot be over-estimated, particularly at a time when there is increasing nervousness about the place of baptism in the life of the Church. It may well be true that in times past we were too lax, and tended to baptize anything that moved. But there is a strong case for arguing that the pendulum has gone far too far in the other direction. And it is a sobering thought to contemplate the narrative of Jesus' own baptism, with all the richness of the experience – heaven opens, the Spirit descends on him, and the voice of God is heard in all its power and reticence – only for this wonderful moment to lead straight into nothing less than *temptation*! We easily overlook what this is really saying, especially if we are smug about a watertight baptism policy, which requires a great deal of suburban articulacy before ever the child is allowed near the font. Surely the message of the gospel itself is clear enough: Jesus' own ministry *began* with his baptism, and was not the result of having his whole message and identity well sewn up in advance.

It may well be that the numbers of infants being brought to baptism will continue to decline, and those of older people coming to baptism after an experience of faith will, proportionately, rise. But we are in danger of denying the free grace of the gospel. The sheer imperative to baptize on the authority of Jesus, with the promise of his presence among us for ever (we do not have to try to be him on his behalf), seems to be supremely compatible with the promise of Emmanuel, who was himself baptized, and then went on his own to think hard about what God wanted him to do. Jesus did not wait until he was somehow 'ready' for baptism. (Remember, John the Baptist was himself more than a little surprised that Jesus should come forward, and perhaps Jesus even surprised himself.) Baptism, like eucharist, is not a possession of the Church, but a sacrament of God's grace. And, like the eucharist, it is intrinsically connected with the forgiveness of sins – if only we will let forgiveness into the picture.

Baptism enriched

It is amazing to think of the different ways in which baptism has been celebrated down the ages. For many years now, I have taken confirmation candidates – and ordinands and students studying the history of the liturgy – through a mime-drama in which some of these different styles are represented. It has always been a source of satisfaction to see their faces light up as they go through the actions (and the dressing up!) that go with these historic scenes. They assimilate much more than they would if I asked them to read ten textbooks. For example, one could travel in a time-machine to Jerusalem in the late fourth century and share with a group of adults the experience of being baptized during the Vigil of Easter, a service that by all accounts used to last all night. The candidates have spent up to three years attending only the first part of the eucharist, when they are dismissed before the sharing of the Peace. Now, at last, they are being led to the baptistery to be dunked in water and anointed with oil; and only then are they taken into the eucharistic assembly. What a strong line of demarcation between their old life and their new one!

By contrast, we could travel to any mediaeval parish church and gather round a font on an afternoon with family and friends, and watch the local priest 'do' the wee bairn. The service has been adapted in such a way that it can be celebrated on its own. The godparents were a group of people the Church kept on pronouncing about as important for the Christian community, and they therefore were told about their responsibilities at the end.

The idealists inevitably prefer the first scene, and perhaps the romantics prefer the second. But the fact remains that both are around today and both of them inform our approaches to baptism. It is not possible – or desirable – to turn the clock back to the days when baptism was available, as in the mediaeval scene, on consumer demand; the Prayer Book tried to make baptism more 'public' by requiring a congregation. Nor is it possible – or desirable – to recover the days of the early Church, with its supposedly tight organization and powerful discipline.

We have to deal with a mess, because we have inherited different modes and styles of baptism, some of them living together at one and the same time. And, it has to be said, some of the researches into the place of baptism in the early Church reveal a varied picture. For example, Augustine in late fourth-century North Africa adapted the rites through sound pastoral sense to meet the needs of different ages and types of people. But there are, nonetheless, a few pointers from the past that could breathe new life into the way many of us approach the font.

The first is to see baptism and eucharist in a unique relationship. Many of our church buildings, old as well as new, spell this out by making the font almost as prominent as the altar. The days of hole-in-the-corner fonts seem numbered. There is a healthy revulsion setting in against those little baptismal bowls on small pillars, in favour of larger and bolder constructions. I know an eighteenth-century church whose interior has been immeasurably improved by the simple manoeuvre of re-siting the font half-way up the nave against the south wall. Architecture is often far more powerful than simply altering the words of the liturgy. When I first saw that font in its new position I immediately thought of some words of a great seventeenth-century preacher, Herbert Thorndike, who once wrote that 'the celebration of the eucharist is the renewal of the covenant of grace'. And on more than one occasion he maintained that we *enter* and *begin* that covenant of grace in baptism.

Covenant is an age-old way of describing our relationship with God, one which has two sides to it. The trouble is that there is a temptation to turn God's overarching initiative of love and forgiveness into a specific, demanding piece of arm-twisting. And so the People of God spend a great deal of their time, or so it would seem, turning that covenant of *grace* into a covenant of *works*, whereby we are actually required to do certain things – or else. To describe baptism as the means whereby we actually enter upon this relationship is to say that it is God's free gift. It is a washing away of sin, a rebirth in a fountain of divine life, a dying to our old life and a rising to a new one. Where we so frequently go wrong is when we start making precise statements about requirements. The font is where we are washed, and the table is where we are fed. And washing and feeding always imply renewal, renewal of perspective, renewal of self-knowledge, renewal of vision, and renewal of love. To enter the covenant of grace at the font and to renew it at the eucharist is the fundamentally Christian way to live.

But it never happens once and for all. My whole life is a constant returning to the font, and I need the food of heaven week by week at God's altar. I have spent much of my adult life grappling with the fact that every time I attend a baptism, my own baptismal promises made on my behalf by my godparents are renewed. And this is simply and solely because God gives me the grace to do just that. When I think about this baptismal life, I know full well that I am part of a slice of Christian history that is having to relearn the same truth. We have been far too individualistic for far too long about baptism. We have thought that baptism is only something we do to someone else, instead of being a mystery in which each one of us is growing all the time. That is why it is so important for Christians regularly to attend baptisms, in the same way that attending marriages sharpens our commitment to the wedding vows, and attending ordinations does the same for those who have made these promises.

All of this means that our liturgies do need to change from time to time to express some of these old truths as they are brought into the present. Perhaps the renunciations need to be a bit more full-blooded than simply being asked 'Do you turn to Christ? Do you repent of your sins? Do you renounce evil?' For baptism is, above all, the beginning of a journey. That is why the language of companionship lies behind the formula being proposed for use at the point in the baptism service when the candidate is signed with the cross:

> Receive the sign of the cross,
> the mark of Christ crucified.

(here the candidates are signed with the cross by the priest, and, if desired, by the sponsors)

> **Walk with us in the life of the Spirit,**
> **As disciples of Christ,**
> **And heirs of God's promise.**

Such language, too, plays an important part in enabling us to see baptism not just as a 'memorial' of Christ's baptism, but as a looking forward to the future, an 'invoking' of God's presence and forgiving grace on Christian life and witness that is to come.

Forgiveness enriched

So much for baptism. What of forgiveness? So far we have considered the place of the font in the total life of the Christian community, in the full knowledge that baptism conveys the grace of God in our lives. But we all know that this, though far richer in its symbolism and language than many of us ever thought, is not quite enough. Forgiveness of sins is the heart of the gospel. It is Christ's Easter gift to the disciples, to the Church, to all people (John 20.22–23). It is therefore a responsibility which all followers of Christ hold, to a greater or lesser extent. And I want to suggest two fresh approaches to it, though I am conscious that neither is startlingly original.

The first approach is to get the perspective right. Forgiveness of sins is proclaimed at baptism: 'repent, and be baptised every one of you in the name of Jesus Christ for the forgiveness of your sins' (Acts 2.38). It is given, too, at the eucharist: 'for this is my blood of the new covenant, which is poured out for many for the forgiveness of sins' (Matthew 26.28). It is mediated by preaching: 'you are already made clean by the word which I have spoken to you' (John 15.3). And it is closely associated with prayer: 'Is any among you sick? Let him call for the elders of the church, and let them pray over him; and if he has committed sins, he will be forgiven' (James 5.14–15). If we want to speak of specific forms of declaring God's forgiveness, we need to see that forgiveness within that wider context.

The second approach is to try to engage with where people are today. Sin is laughed at – and probably always has been. Sin is taken for granted, because it is part of being human. There is a lot of confusion about what exactly constitutes a sin, and ours is by no means the first age to lack a sense of clarity in some areas. Perhaps we have been too clear about individual kinds of sins, and have underrated the social and the global. Which offends God more – wilful adultery that breaks a marriage or an oil-slick that destroys animal life? My hunch is that people nowadays see sin more in terms of *addiction* than anything else: 'I just can't help doing that'; 'I said the same offensive thing to John yet again'; 'I feel helpless in the face of a life that's getting on top of me.' Our sense of personal isolation can be such that we feel alone in an alien world. I shall never forget introducing two parishioners to each other in the same week that both had been brutally and suddenly sacked.

Both were in shock and feeling bitter. Straight after the eucharist, they shook hands, and the words 'bear one another's burdens' (Galatians 6.2) took on a new meaning.

How do these two approaches converge? Forgiveness is never a gift that can be neatly packaged. It can be very near the bone: realizing that bearing a grudge isn't really worth it any longer; or coming to the knowledge that I am not after all the perfect human being I would like to be. In the face of a culture that is, on the surface, too casual about sin, it would be tempting to go in the other direction and become too scrupulous and particular. Anglicans have long held that private confession is an important ministry for those with troubled consciences. Tucked away in the Visitation of the Sick in the old Prayer Book is a form of private confession and absolution. I wish more people availed themselves of this right, but often shyness – and perhaps distrust of the clergy and old fears about popery! – gets in the way. Not all priests are gifted in the personal ministry of speaking the appropriate words to the penitent before giving the absolution. But those are not really good enough excuses. My own experience, both as a penitent and as a parish priest, convinces me that there is no shortage of problems people want to talk about. Sometimes the conversation may lead into formal confession, on other occasions it will develop into a sense that the person concerned is going to pray and think hard and try to put the matter right.

But there are, I think, two other ways whereby some convergence may be made between the work of the Church and the experience of individuals. One is to draw attention to what is already there in the liturgy, in the introduction to the confession, the confession itself, and the absolution. The trouble with organized religion is that it can often be its own worst enemy, formality and routine worship being top of that particular list. In the eucharist, the confession usually comes at the start, perhaps when people are a little breathless with things because to come into the presence of God is to be confronted by our need for forgiveness and renewal. Or it may come later, when they have had time to be challenged by the Word of God read, preached on, and prayed about. In either position (and I am inclined to prefer the earlier place), this little triad of invitation, saying sorry and being forgiven, provide an example of how the practice of forgiving and being forgiven can become part of one's life. It won't necessarily make us *better* people but might make us more honest! But there is a good chance that it will make us more *contented* with ourselves, one another and God. The invitation is God's free gift, the confession is our response, the absolution is the seal on what has already been given. To make more of this perhaps means being more ready (but when are we really ready for God?), and a period of silence helps. But that invitation is now one of the places in the service where the president can improvise, and would that more presidents prepared these more carefully! A perceptive friend of mine composed this invitation, which puts us and God in our places, and depicts God in terms of the one who cannot be anything other than the loving father:

> Let us remember the week that is past,
> its sweetness and its disappointments,
> the struggles within us
> and the knowledge that God is longing to welcome us home.

God is longing to welcome us home: from the weakness of a fallen human nature, from intended slights, from uncompleted tasks, from unworthy thoughts and fantasies. All of that God shares – and has redeemed. To keep going back with the same old sins is only depressing if we fail to unite our confession with a growing self-awareness that in spite of the weaknesses, God is still prepared to bless us, and to use the mess in his purposes of love. Often the real obstacle to forgiveness is pride, our reluctance to let our sins go.

Another avenue worth exploring in order to try to draw together the fact of forgiveness and the way people are is to ask what may be missing from our public liturgies. One of the principles underlying the composition of the various new rites was to 'strip down' a 'cluttered' service in order that it might speak more clearly. This may be one of the reasons why some people find the new services move somewhat angularly from one thing to another – a bit like a car trying to change gear by double-declutch, instead of a more smooth movement. People will often tell you most eloquently what is missing when they have to write prayers themselves. In many churches, the intercessions are now in the hands of the laity, which means that the clergy have to do the listening. What do we find ourselves faced with? Under the surface, there is often a desire for devotional prayers that reflect on the experience of faith in a personal manner. I wonder how much this is being listened to by clergy, to say nothing of the professional liturgists who are going to be revising the Alternative Service Book. If the liturgy really is the work of the people (which is what it means), and if it is therefore their possession (and not the clergy's), then these indirect hints need to be heeded. One of the devotional prayers I have heard used at the end of the intercessions is a kind of extended comment on much of what I have been trying to say. It is a prayer that was originally written by Archbishop Michael Ramsey for a service book at Repton, where he went to school:

> Jesus, Lord and Master, who served your disciples in
>   washing their feet;
> serve us often, serve us daily, in washing our motives,
>   our ambitions, our actions;
> that we may share with you in your mission to the world,
> and serve others gladly for your sake; to whom be glory
>   for ever.

Foot-washing

In John's account of the Last Supper, there is no narrative of the institution of the eucharist. Instead, John inserts an account of Jesus turning all convention upside down by washing the feet of the disciples after the meal is over (John 13.1–11). Foot-washing is a necessary part of the culture in which Jesus lived – bare feet get very dirty and dusty on the way to a meal in someone else's home. But it soon became a ceremony of profound power that eventually found its place in the Maundy Thursday eucharist. Our own age has seen a revival of the custom. And I have often been asked, what is its exact meaning?

There can be no 'exact' meaning. Foot-washing tells us about
God in Christ Jesus. So it is part example of humility, part our
being strengthened and sanctified, and part our being enabled
to walk out and onward with the good news of salvation for all.
But each of these three qualities of Jesus' ministry is about
forgiveness. Humility, sanctification and mission, all these have
to start with ourselves, as weak, yet made strong, as proud, yet
made humble, and as trying so hard to have hearts of stone
when God wants us to work away with him at refining hearts of
flesh. Some of this comes across in a modern hymn by Brian
Wren, focused strongly in the following verses:

> Great God, in Christ you call our name,
> and then receive us as your own,
> not through some merit, right or claim,
> but by your gracious love alone.
> We strain to glimpse your mercy-seat,
> and find you kneeling at our feet.
>
> Then take the towel, and break the bread,
> and humble us, and call us friends.
> Suffer and serve till all are fed,
> and show how grandly love intends
> to work till all creation sings,
> to fill all worlds, to crown all things.

4

☙☙☙

Access to the meal

Part 1

The eucharist is a public service of proclamation and thanks-giving. It essentially involves a communion of people gathering together for prayer and thanksgiving and is not a private or individual act of worship. Yet in practice, that communion of people can often be limited merely to the community of faith, those people who actively believe and regularly worship. The eucharist is in danger of becoming a very 'churchy' service which is understood only by the initiated. This would be a great loss. Whereas it may be right that only those formally initiated into the Church (that is, baptized, and maybe, confirmed) should receive the bread and wine, it is certainly right that all should be able to participate in the eucharist. Everyone does this by becoming a part of the proclamation and thanksgiving. All 'sit under' the Word of God, hear the story of God and find for themselves a place within that story. Then all, with their work, their concerns and their joys, become part of the offering to God which is made in the great prayer of thanksgiving.

However, the experience that is commonly voiced by those not actively involved in church life is that the Church is slowly privatizing itself. Many have said that, although they could not understand and did not like the service of Matins, at least everyone could take part. This is an important comment, for it expresses the public nature of religion. People felt that the things of God played a part in their lives, even if it was on the boundary, and that they had ready access to God as and when they wanted it. Therefore many churches responded to this by creating a service of ready access, the so-called 'family service', whilst maintaining the regular diet of weekly eucharists. A few years later, the vicar and PCC realize the difficulty of helping people make the transition from a monthly family service to a more frequent eucharist. It seems that a large part of the family service congregation is stuck in that particular type of worship. There is an intuitive sense that communion is for the 'in crowd', the worthy or the righteous. This sense appals those on the inside and leaves them feeling very uncomfortable. Some manage this discomfort by wanting to draw clearer boundaries between those who are fully initiated and those who have yet to make a commitment. But others want to affirm both their own discipleship and also a ready access for those who do not yet show such commitment.

This issue of the public accessibility of Christian worship is most often raised in the form of a discussion about the Established Church. For the Church of England is seen some-how to belong not to the members (whatever way they are defined) but to everyone. There are those in the Church of England who are tired of the constraints that come with this public perception of what it is to be the national church. There are those in all denominations who feel that the free proclama-tion of the gospel of Jesus Christ is compromised by any asso-ciation with power and pomp that is a natural part of national, political life. Moreover many voices are being raised in other quarters saying that as our country is no longer predominantly Christian, the Church should not have a special place in national life. Indeed, some go further to say that the Church's public presence is oppressive, moralistic and unsuitable for a modern age. Many want the Church and State to divorce one another and be free to lead separate lives. I am strongly opposed to such a divorce.

The Church of England has recently developed a nasty habit of becoming introspective. Especially when under stress or attack from outside, the Church, like other institutions, becomes concerned only with its own internal life. So synod meetings become more and more burdened with discussions of reorganization and finance, and have less time to devote to theology and the vision of God. If in the end the Church of England were to cut loose its established obligations to the State, religious people could find that there was less that was drawing them out of their own religious concerns. But God does not belong to religious people and the commands of God are not merely for those who pray and seek holiness in their lives. So the Church of England, with other churches, has declared a Decade of Evangelism, ten years of turning outwards beyond our own boundaries, of speaking forth the gospel with all its promise, hope and demands.

Yet within this ten-year programme there is a trap. To encourage new people to take God seriously the message is presented as one of choosing: 'You have to make a choice. You can turn to God. You can receive the blessings and promise of salvation in Jesus Christ.' But that is only one part of the truth, namely, that we can choose to follow God in Jesus Christ. There is another aspect that says that the commands of God are valid and right, whether we choose them or not. The claims of Godly living reach beyond those who are interested in God, and embrace us all. Thus we all know that lasting peace will only be established by forgiving and restoring our enemies. This is a public truth though there are many ways of bringing it into effect, and the Christian would want to go on to the point of loving the enemies. We all know that a stable society requires us to honour those who have gone before us ('our fathers and mothers'), to maintain good opinions of others ('not bearing false witness') and to limit acquisitiveness (by 'not coveting our neighbours' possessions'). These statements, often summarized as the Ten Commandments, are public truths and not private choices. They are a matter of general obligations and not only individual commitment.

Just as God does not belong to the Church, so also public life does not belong merely to those interested in politics. The example that brings this home to me is my daily listening to the

Today programme on Radio 4. At times I listen avidly to local and national figures talking about matters of significance. Then sometimes, in a flash, I am struck by the irrelevance of it all. Politicians seem to be speaking to other politicians, not to the public, about ideas that they choose to say are important. Yet it seems that they and their work have lost contact with daily living.

Now, I have heard teachers say that running a school would be easy if only they did not have any children to teach! I have said myself that leading a parish would be simple if only I did not have any parishioners. But it is a dangerous joke to make to say that politicians would get on so much better if only they did not have to listen to or meet with the public. Political life essentially belongs to the public. It is the place for considering public truths, for fulfilling public obligations and for ordering the public good. Just as the things of God are too important to leave to the Church, public life is too important to hand over to politicians. Many forces in society are pulling us in the direction of separation and compartmentalization. The establishment of the Church of England is an important stand against these forces, simply because it crosses boundaries.

An important consequence of this is that the Church's worship must be accessible to all. Those who have already heeded the Decade of Evangelism have probably reformed their worship to be open and user-friendly. Newcomers are made to feel at ease in an unfamiliar building and have the service explained to them by an experienced worshipper as it goes along. Invitations to join in home groups will be made over coffee after the service. However, we are falling into the trap of the Decade if we are only seeking to draw people into the fellowship of the church, because we are implying that the gospel only has something to offer those who are committed to it. We need to regain our confidence that the gospel speaks to those who have some belief or none. We need to trust that it is worth people hearing the proclamation that happens within worship, whether they return for more or not.

At a recent civic service attended both by the parish

congregation and by the local mayor and councillors, the first reading was from Philippians, chapter 4:

> Finally, beloved, whatever is true, whatever is honourable, whatever is just, whatever is pure, whatever is pleasing, whatever is commendable, if there is any excellence and if there is anything worthy of praise, think about these things. Keep on doing the things that you have learned and received and heard and seen in me, and the God of peace will be with you.

This is a brilliant and poetic summary of our common public obligation. We all have to seek after truth, purity and excellence, and seek out things worthy of honour and praise. When we find them, we need to dwell on them within so that we ourselves become people of truth, purity and excellence. This is required of us all whether we are in the Church or public life, and we are strengthened by doing it together. The Church has a right and a responsibility to present this as part of the gospel that will inspire and direct all people. At times the Christian preacher will also want to expand the understanding of what makes up truth, purity and excellence by reference to stories about who Jesus was and what he did. Yet it is clear that the proclamation that happens in all worship, and that is an essential part of the eucharist, can and must be public and accessible for all.

However, it is when we turn our attention to the other main aspect of the eucharist as a public service of thanksgiving that we encounter greater difficulties. Colin Buchanan, a persistent objector to the establishment of the Church of England, has recently written:

> [We need] a credible way of ceasing to pretend that the state is Christian, and with that a realistic way of recognising that society around us is not Christian. Once that is clear, then a committed basis for membership and a willingness to call unbelief unbelief give the right springboard for mission.

His programme is to be able to identify a committed membership which includes a readiness to exclude unbelievers. This will then provide motivation for mission. Yet all is based on a straightforward evaluation of the non-Christian nature of society. This programme seems disarmingly simple but is too narrowly based. It would further privatize the Church's worship, drive members into a ghetto, and make many ordinary people lose touch with their spiritual lives. It is too much focused on the internal needs of the Church and not enough on the breadth of God's kingdom.

It will be helpful to describe another situation from a different time and context. In Jesus' day the Jews lived in a society that was very clearly not ordered exactly as they wished, for the Romans had overall control. However, much of the regular administration was delegated and, for the most part, Jews were free to live in accordance with their beliefs. There was a wide range of beliefs and religious practices and this was an advantage of Roman occupation. For no party could take over the country and impose their interpretation of the Law on others. All Jews could be said to live in accordance with the Law, accepting a lot of variety and interpretation, except those who actively flouted it. These the gospels refer to as 'tax-collectors and sinners'. The term 'sinners' is a very strong term and does not merely refer to those who broke the Law unintentionally or from weakness.

Although the common people kept the Law, there were those who wanted to live a more dedicated life of obedience and holiness. Some took on for themselves the purity laws that only priests were required to keep. Some accepted stricter interpretations of laws which restricted their daily lifestyle and symbolized a greater offering to God. These Jews formed themselves into various groups each with its own emphasis, but all aiming to serve God fully. The precise historical evidence is quite thin but the most commonly known party was the Pharisees. What is clear is that the Pharisees did not despise the common people *en bloc*, nor did they believe that the common people were excluded from salvation. Most of the rigorist parties still believed that salvation from God was for all Jews within the covenant. It is only at a later date that exclusivist parties developed whose beliefs restricted salvation merely to their own group. In Jesus' day the Pharisees would not have imposed their own lifestyle on others, but would have rejoiced when any Jew felt called to join their party. This is not how Pharisees are commonly understood. However, it gives a remarkable picture that combines religious tolerance and commitment which is instructive for us today.

It is not right to draw simple parallels between this period in history and our own day, for there are so many differences in the ways people lived and the expectations of society. However, this description prompts us to question the three parts of Buchanan's programme and therefore to affirm the public nature of the eucharist as celebrated today.

We see that it is possible to practise religious commitment and enthusiasm without having to call weak belief unbelief. The Pharisees developed their own drive to holiness because they considered that it was a right offering to God, and maintained it (presumably) because they experienced it as holy living. They did not rely on knowing that they were in the community of salvation and others were excluded to act as a motivation in their religious lives. Indeed, they still valued the common people as children of the covenant and yet could also recognize that 'tax-collectors and sinners' had counted themselves out. There is here a readiness to value tentative religious belief and practice for what it is, as well as a longing to reform individual lives.

The great difference between the situation of the first-century Jews as described and our own is that as a nation we do not believe that we belong as a whole people to the covenant people of God. There was that belief in first-century Judaism that included everyone apart from 'the tax-collectors and sinners'. However, there still is a very widespread belief in our country today that people belong to the Church unless they positively dissociate themselves from it. There are good historical reasons for this belief that lie in the work of genera-tions of Christians providing baptism, teaching and worship for all. The theological support for this is found in the belief that all men and women are created in the image of God, and that God is drawing people to himself both within and outside the boundaries of the Church. Clearly we know that a good percentage of the population belong to other religions or actively distance themselves from the Christian faith. But there is no reason to feel that by valuing the general interest shown in the Christian God, we therefore undermine the explicit commitment of those who actively seek God in Jesus Christ.

The second part of Buchanan's programme is an evaluation of the non-Christian nature of society. The first-century Jews both knew themselves to be living under pagan control and also considered themselves still as a nation serving God. We too can easily recognize that our society is in need of reformation. The Church should be actively involved with those in power to amend our public life to be more in accordance with God's will. Yet if we look carefully, we can also see how Christian virtues are woven deep into the fabric of society. It is this that people intuitively recognize and look to the Church to maintain and protect.

This is the springboard for the Christian's mission. We are called to remind people that they live under God's rule. By retelling the story of God's love that has been made known to us in the past, we focus people's attention on what is already amongst us, albeit at times quite hidden. This is combined with a call to reform our common life in the future. This all has validity because we have already begun that reformation in our own lives. We are not held up as perfect examples but we are witnesses to the experience of God's transforming grace. Thereby we have the right mixture of commitment without exclusion for individuals, and reformation for the future combined with appreciation of the past for society. This is what is and must be found in every celebration of the eucharist.

So we see the public nature of the eucharist even in the ministry of the sacrament, the part that centres on the great prayer of thanksgiving. It is this part of the service above all that can seem merely to involve those who are committed and to be dedicated to their feeding and nurture. Indeed, at certain times in history this was the case. Yet there are various ways available

for everyone to participate in the thanksgiving. We have already
seen in Chapters 2 and 3 how the eucharistic prayer can involve
others by being a retelling of their spiritual story. We have just
seen how this can be true for the nation as well as individuals.
We will see in Chapter 7, by exploring the nature of 'offering',
how all worshippers, baptized or not, can be enabled to participate in the eucharist. For now I wish to concentrate on one
very practical part of the service when physically there seems to
be a division between those who are and those who are not part
of the community of faith.

After the eucharistic prayer, the breaking of the bread and the
Lord's Prayer, the president invites people forward to receive
the now consecrated bread and wine.

> Draw near with faith. Receive the body of our Lord Jesus Christ
> which he gave for you, and his blood which he shed for you.

> Eat and drink in remembrance that he died for you, and feed on
> him in your hearts by faith with thanksgiving.

The president will be aware that some visitors or occasional
worshippers may not want to receive communion or, according
to the discipline of the Church, are not in a position to receive
communion. Thus many presidents will begin with an explanation of who can and who cannot receive. In addition, for those
unfamiliar with the regular practice of that particular church
(whether people receive standing or kneeling, whether people
receive the bread in their hands or on their tongues, etc.), there
is often a need for stage directions. All this serves to increase
anxiety for the occasional worshipper, and although the
message is 'draw near with faith', what may be heard is 'come
here only if you are quite sure what to do'. I have great sympathy
for presidents at this time, for it is very difficult to give a brief
positive message without using a phrase such as 'if you are not
going to receive communion . . .'. This only serves to isolate
and prevent participation.

If this is so, then more time and work needs to be given to
this crucial moment so that the vital theme of public thanksgiving is not undermined. Isaiah, chapter 55, begins:

1. Ho, everyone who thirsts,
   come to the waters;
   and you that have no money,
   come, buy and eat!
   Come, buy wine and milk
   without money and without price.
2. Why do you spend your money for that which is not bread,
   and your labour for that which does not satisfy?
   Listen carefully to me, and eat what is good,
   and delight yourselves in rich food.
3. Incline your ear, and come to me;
   listen, so that you may live;
   I will make with you an everlasting covenant,
   my steadfast, sure love for David.
4. See, I made him a witness to the peoples,
   a leader and commander for the peoples.
5. See, you shall call nations that you do not know,
   and nations that do not know you shall run to you,
   because of the Lord your God, the Holy One of Israel,
   for he has glorified you.
6. Seek the Lord while he may be found,
   call upon him while he is near;
7. let the wicked forsake their way,
   and the unrighteous their thoughts;
   let them return to the Lord, that he may have mercy on them,
   and to our God, for he will abundantly pardon.

This is the climax of the second part of the book of Isaiah which is found in chapters 40 to 55. In the name of God, the prophet clearly and forcefully invites the people 'to come', 'to buy and eat' and 'to come and listen'. All who thirst are invited without assessing qualification of merit. The style is based on a market-seller's cry but, even so, money is not needed. Clearly the prophet is not speaking from himself but naming the offer from God which is freely given. Earlier in these chapters, the prophet calls the people to take part in the moment of deliverance, the act of God that was freeing his people from exile. But in this climax, a further move is made and an invitation calls people to share in the consequence of deliverance, that is, present salvation. The prophet also balances the call to the individual (v. 1) with the outcome for the nation (v. 5). Thus the parts fit together: God has delivered, everyone is called to enjoy the fruits of this, and the consequence is that God will use the people to draw others. What a combination of individual commitment, common experience and a motivation to mission! Of course, the prophet is not blind to the importance of sin, seen either as chasing after emptiness (v. 2) or turning against righteousness (v. 7). But the call is to 'come'!

I find in this passage a knitting together of the themes found in this chapter. The salvation of God is, in the words of the eucharist, made known and offered to all who come to hear. Our practice must match this so that those who seek and call upon the Lord will indeed find him.

Part 2

The holy in our midst

> The gifts of God for the people of God.
> **Jesus Christ is holy,**
> **Jesus Christ is Lord,**
> **to the glory of God the Father.**

These words are sometimes recited just before communion in the Rite A eucharist of the Alternative Service Book. They read – and recite – well at one level. But what do they actually mean? What is so special about the president saying that God's gifts are for his people, and the congregation asserting that Jesus is Lord, to the glory of God the Father? As usual, a little bit of history helps. This formula is, in fact, an adaptation of a cry by the president in exactly the same position in all the Eastern liturgies since the fourth century. 'Holy things for holy persons', says the priest. To which the reply comes, 'One is the holy, Jesus Christ, to the glory of God the Father'. It is as if there is an argument going on. The bread and wine, now conse-crated, are holy – and so must those be who dare to approach. But the people argue back that there is only one person who is really holy, Jesus Christ, and his holiness is for the glory of God the Father.

This little argument demonstrates one of the fundamental paradoxes about the eucharist: the holy in our midst. Here is God, the great and mighty one, taking upon himself the form of a servant, as Paul expresses it in what may be part of an early Christian hymn:

> Have this mind among yourselves, which you have in Christ Jesus, who, though he was in the form of God, did not count equality with God a thing to be grasped, but emptied himself, taking the form of a servant, being born in the likeness of men. And being found in human form he humbled himself and became obedient unto death, even death on a cross. Therefore God has highly exalted him and bestowed on him the name which is above every name, that at the name of Jesus every knee should bow, in heaven and on earth and under the earth, and every tongue confess that Jesus Christ is Lord, to the glory of God the Father. (Philippians 2.5–11)

If we are to make any sense of this God-in-our-midst, we are bound to feel both the intimacy of Jesus' words and deeds as they make themselves real in our hearts and lives, and also the distance of the Holy One, who lives and reigns in heaven. Or, to put it in more direct terms, if our life is a search for meaning, then that meaning is bound to be elusive, because life is a mixture of getting it right and getting it wrong, of understanding what it is all about, and of getting the wrong end of the stick. If we identify that 'meaning' with God – which is not far from what the fourth gospel expresses by 'the Word' (John 1.1ff.) – then our God is going to be a mixture of the obvious and the mysterious.

Once we place these observations within the eucharist, we have embarked on a course with a similar mixture of certainties and uncertainties. Indeed, this life of faith is by its nature a walk in which we do not always make the journey by sight. Jeremy Taylor, one of the great devotional writers of the seventeenth century, expresses our life in God thus:

> For as God descended and came into the tabernacle invested with a cloud, so Christ comes to meet us clothed with a mystery; He

hath a house below as well as above; here is His dwelling and here are His provisions, here is His fire and here His meat; hither God sends His Son, and here His Son manifests Himself; the church and the holy table of the Lord, the assemblies of the saints, and the devotions of His people, the word and the sacrament, the oblation of bread and wine and the offering of ourselves, the consecration and the communion, are the things of God and of Jesus Christ, and he that is employed in these is there where God loves to be, and where Christ is to be found; in the employments in which God delights, in the ministries of His own choice, in the work of the gospel and the methods of grace, in the economy of heaven and the dispensations of eternal happiness.

Taylor loved to speak in terms of heaven and earth, the mysterious wrapped in a cloud and yet visible among us, and the place of the Church's sacraments within that divine frame-work. Put in practical terms – and Taylor was a practical writer – this means that the eucharist is always going to walk a tension through the lives of those who reflect upon this central sacrament. One of the most crucial of these points of tension concerns access to the table itself. Who is worthy? No one. Who is really ready? Not one of us. Who dares to approach? Hardly anyone, if any at all. And yet the Church keeps celebrating the eucharist, keeps inviting communicants to 'draw near with faith', persists in offering the eucharist in countless interests and contexts, but continually aware that there are always going to be those who will not wish or feel able to 'draw near'. At a time when the eucharist is being celebrated with more frequency, and with (proportionately) more communicants than has been the case for centuries, we cannot fail to observe the numerical decline of membership in many parts of the Western world. And this poses the question: is the Church becoming a eucharistic ghetto?

Public relations for the eucharist?

There has, in fact, always been a tension between sacramental and non-sacramental worship right down through the ages. When the cry 'holy things for holy persons' was introduced into the Eastern Churches, there was a danger that people would come forward without due preparation. After the early centuries of persecution, it suddenly became respectable to be a Christian. The Church went public, even took over many large, secular buildings for worship and other church activities, and there came a resultant need to handle these large crowds. There had long been a custom of dismissing those preparing for baptism at the end of the first part of the eucharist, so that they would not even see the bread and wine placed on the altar, let alone the consecration and distribution. That effectively sliced the service in half. And along with the unbaptized there also went the 'penitents', a class of people who had committed grievous sins, and who were – temporarily – excluded from sharing in the eucharist.

But people also began to do something else – they would stay for the eucharist, but not receive the sacrament, even though they were baptized. It may well be that the cry 'holy things for holy persons' actually encouraged such a trend, or else that its introduction could have been its liturgical counterpart. We are not worthy, but we are still going to hang around! Moreover, as the eucharist migrated from the big, communal celebration in a large basilica, like San Clemente in Rome, to the small side-chapel of a monastery, the popular perception of the service altered. The priest would celebrate the service largely silently, assisted by a server, and the congregation might be there or might not be there. The sense of the holy in our midst would still be ever present. But the practice of non-participation developed further and further, until, in the later Middle Ages, people had to be encouraged to receive communion at least four times a year. It did not help matters that they were required to go to private confession to a priest first. 'Participation' in the eucharist came to consist in being present, praying, enjoying the actions and the symbolism – but not eating the bread (the chalice had been withdrawn, for health and other reasons) more than a few times in the year.

The Reformation sought to redress this balance. Worship was simplified, the bread and wine were eaten and drunk from 'ordinary-looking' ware. The services were translated into the language of the people. But for all the encouragement given by the authorities and the theologians to more frequent communion, the sheer weight of custom on the whole prevailed. To take one example, the Diaries of Parson Woodforde in his eighteenth-century vicarage of Weston in Norfolk reveal the practice of communion four times a year, at Christmas, Easter, Pentecost and at the in-gathering of the harvest. In the same century, Methodists were advocating frequent communion; John Wesley himself received the sacrament every Sunday throughout his life, and also on weekdays too. The main difference between Catholic and Protestant worship in this regard is that Catholics went to mass but did not have to receive communion, whereas Protestants of all types only had a eucharist when there were communicants in addition to the celebrant.

Our own century has seen a drastic revision of this scene, with frequent communion actively encouraged by nearly all church leaders. I can remember discussions in our local church when I was a boy about making the eucharist the main Sunday service, and displacing Morning Prayer. We were accused of being 'high church' by the older members, who felt that familiarity might breed contempt. But the innovators eventually won through.

We are thus faced with an important dilemma, which Richard Holloway has recently expressed in terms of setting the eucharistic table and making it glorious with all the resources available to us, but of neglecting to gather the people in. The cry 'holy things for holy persons' rings in our ears, reminding us of the wonder of the Word made flesh. The complexities of history serve as a laxative for our fears that we are the first generation ever to deal with this matter – we are clearly not.

Lateral thinking might help

Access to the eucharistic table has always been through the font. But in the West, an additional rite, that of confirmation, developed in the Middle Ages. In origin, it was simply the concluding part of the baptism service, in which the candidate is anointed with chrism (a sweet-smelling oil). In time it developed other features, including the laying-on of hands, and, at the Reformation, the candidate's own, conscious renewal of baptismal vows. Anglicans retained the restriction of confirmation to bishops at the Reformation, and the practice of many parts of the mediaeval Church of insisting on confirmation before communion. Nowadays, Roman Catholics increasingly delegate confirmation to priests, with chrism blessed by the bishop. Presbyterians, Methodists and Lutherans have always practised confirmation by the local minister. None of the Eastern Churches has ever had confirmation; the anointing with chrism invariably is given with baptism, hence their practice of infant communion. Another mess all round!

But history should not unnerve us here. It seems clear that confirmation has never had a single, logical role. On the other hand, to jettison it altogether would undermine so many structures of church life and practice that people would be left confused. The Church of England, like many others, seems uncertain about the age of confirmation. Those who are pressing for communion at an early age are often encouraged to present candidates for confirmation then, whereas others want early communion and a delayed confirmation, resulting in a rite of commitment in late teens, at the earliest.

These complex issues cannot be ignored. But I suspect that what is going on under the surface is something much more interesting. We are probably moving into an era in which *baptism* is going to be seen as the entry into the Church – and the eucharistic table. It may well be that it will require undergirding of one sort or another, such as teaching and instruction, time for reflection and prayer. These are all increasingly part and parcel of ordinary Christian living. We are no longer – if we ever were – in the kind of situation where people are baptized as infants, confirmed later on, and then taken to communion and left to their own devices and desires. Confirmation will remain, but it will adapt, as it has already, to include other needs, such as welcoming Christians from other Churches (without denying the reality of their previous Christian life), and giving an opportunity for those who have experienced a renewal of faith to be reaffirmed in their Christian discipleship. Both these constituencies are likely to grow over the years and it is important that they are not ignored. They are part of the 'up-side' of an age of ecclesiastical pluralism.

Another area for exploration is the notion of participation. There is a kind of superficiality that regards access to anything as the right of anyone, and once that access has been given, life can continue and the next hurdle can be broken through. To put it rather bluntly, we are rife with rights, but with neither mysteries nor responsibilities!

The trouble is that participating in the life of God cannot be reduced to the level of mere access. As Richard Hooker, one of the founding Fathers of Anglicanism, wrote at the end of the sixteenth century, 'The divine mystery is more true than plain'. And he goes on to say with telling firmness: 'Participation is that mutual inward hold which Christ hath of us and we of him.' Hooker loved the language of participation. Indeed, it is a keyword throughout his entire discussion of the eucharist in his great masterpiece, *Treatise on the Laws of Ecclesiastical Polity*. For him, participation is the way in which the life of God is shared with the lives of human beings. It is not the mere walking through a gate-post, the breaching of a barrier, the winning of another prize. Perhaps we have turned the eucharist into baptism by negligent frequency. Once we've done it, we've done it, and that is the end of the story. Participation is about the capacity to go back again and again to be fed, and to be ready to see something new and creative in the life of God as that continues to be shared. Our access to the table is the access of repeated, devout feeding. I was once interviewed by a journalist and asked what I would say to a person who came to my church for the first time and wanted to talk about it afterwards. I replied that I would say something along the following lines: 'I hope you enjoyed it. And I hope you will come again. And I hope, too, that you won't expect the meaning of everything to leap to your ears and eyes at first taking. God is to be enjoyed, and that means being ready for surprises, wonders and subtleties.'

Then there is the question of the 'we' in the prayers at communion. If I have one major criticism of many a modern eucharistic prayer, it is the inbuilt sense that the only group that matters is the congregation in general, and the communicants at that service in particular. The first eucharistic prayer in the Alternative Service Book prays with all the gusto it can manage:

> . . . and as we eat and drink these holy gifts
> in the presence of your divine majesty,
> renew us by your Spirit,
> inspire us with your love,
> and unite us in the body of your Son . . .

The same propensity for introspection is to be seen in many other prayers of this kind. It has even been somewhat irreverently referred to as 'all this wee-ing in the liturgy'! On the other hand, in the old Prayer Book communion rite, the first long prayer after the distribution (sometimes called the prayer of oblation, because it is a prayer of offering) avoids such exclusiveness:

> O Lord and heavenly Father, we thy humble servants entirely desire thy fatherly goodness mercifully to accept this our sacrifice of praise and thanksgiving; most humbly beseeching thee to grant, that by the merits and death of thy Son Jesus Christ, and through faith in his blood, *we and all thy whole Church* may obtain remission of our sins, and all other benefits of his passion. (my italics)

'We and all thy whole Church . . . ' It is a subtle way of reminding the congregation that there are other eucharistic fellowships. It is a yet more subtle way of saying that the Church – by promise – is the whole community. And it is an even more subtle way of pointing to the Church beyond the grave and gate of death. When I took my father's funeral, I prayed 'we and all thy whole Church, with this our brother Eric, may obtain remission of our sins, and all other benefits of his passion'.

One corollary of this observation is to suggest that we don't just pray for the communicants, but that we pray for other concerns towards the end of the eucharistic prayer, including the Church's mission and hopes, as well as its union with the Church in heaven, always a neglected area in an age that seems to have lost interest in the nearer presence of God. If we do not start widening our perspectives, we run the risk of regarding the eucharist as our own private possession. We do not have to protect the eucharist from anyone, except – by sound tradition – from serious offenders. It is we who have to keep hearing the gospel and be renewed by its vital power. If we sit back and think that all is well, in our eucharistic ghetto, keeping it to ourselves, not offering it for all estates of our fellow humans, we fall into the dangerous trap of complacency. The great nineteenth-century Danish hymn-writer Nikolai Grundtvig, in a characteristically direct hymn to the Holy Spirit, prays thus:

> God the Holy Spirit, the one who makes us born again,
> to be the children of him who created us,
> to be everything that Gentile and Jew alike forfeited
> through sin, and lost through death;
> Be our interpreter, be our speech,
> be our heavenly comforter,
> till we become renewed from top to toe!

He is using very ordinary Danish when he prays for renewal 'from top to toe'. And, as if to emphasize this earthiness, the last three lines are repeated in the last verse of the hymn.

An outward-looking culture in the Church does not, of course, mean that the Church can afford to adopt an attitude of triumphalism to the life that surrounds it. In a book written in 1951, called *Christ and Culture*, the theologian Richard Niebuhr suggested various ways in which Christianity has dealt with it. Of the false options, he easily identifies 'Christ against culture' as one which has been most welcome to particular ages of the Church. It is easy to caricature – you hit someone else with Christ. But after examining others, he finally comes up with the voice that seems most gospel-centred – Christ the transformer of culture. Here we have the vision of the Church trusting the Lord, and being the community within the wider community, nurturing the faithful, but empowering them to move out from the eucharistic table and to be God's people on earth, regardless of the response.

Some of the most moving stories of mission have come from groups and communities who have done just that. It may well be that this is the way in which the eucharist has to be changed – though we have the spectre of radical experiments in the 1960s failing to turn back in three seconds the effects of centuries of opposition to the Christian message. Liturgical changes are necessary. The liturgy, unlike the Bible, does not have canonical status. So we must expect it to change, preferably more than every 400 years. But I suspect that the changes made in the liturgy by Christ the transformer of culture will be more slow and organic, more to do with the attitudes of those who come, and less to do with where which bit comes, or sudden dramatic changes to people.

But perhaps the most obvious need is to focus on the sense of the eucharist as a *public* celebration, in which the values and aspirations of the whole community are brought before God for thanksgiving – and judgement. One classic example of this comes from a figure to whom we have already referred, Lancelot Andrewes, who preached before the Court of King James I repeatedly at the major festivals. He had an idiosyncratic style, though he was greatly admired, and 96 of his greatest sermons were published within three years of his death, which took place in 1626 when he was Bishop of Winchester. Adopting a canny approach to his hearers and the events surrounding them, he called them again and again, at the end of his preachings, to come and share in the sacrament, and to walk to heaven. These two concerns walk frequently side by side. In other words, he had a strong sense of the eucharist as a celebration of the *kingdom*, which inevitably gives it a perspective over and above the merely churchy. Like Grundtvig, the Dane, two centuries later, Andrewes can adopt stunningly direct language that strikes at the heart of the human condition, as with this, the final paragraph of his Pentecost sermon at Court in 1613:

Resolve then not to send Him away, on His own day, and nothing done, but to receive His seal, and to dispose ourselves, as pliable and fit to receive it. And then shall we but evil do, nay not at all, unless it please Him to take us in hand and to work as ready for it. To pray Him then so to do, to give us hearts of wax that will receive this impression; and having received it, to give us careful minds withal well to look to it, that it take as little harm as our infirmity will permit. That so we may keep ourselves from this unkind sin of grieving Him That hath been, and is, so good to us. Which the God of mercy grant us, for His Son, and by his Spirit, to Whom . . .

A vigil of prayer

Tuesday, 15 January 1991 will rank as an historic day in the Middle East. It was the United Nations deadline for Iraqi withdrawal from Kuwait, and it marked the beginning of the Gulf War. The churches of Guildford wanted to mark this important day and we eventually decided to hold a vigil of prayer for peace in the oldest place of worship in the town, the church of St Mary, which has a Saxon tower and where people have come to worship and pray for many, many centuries. So, from noon until 3 o'clock in the afternoon, the little church was packed with people, coming and going, to enter into the pain and the anxiety of another international conflict.

The centre of our vigil was a eucharist, which was shared between ministers and laity of several churches, presided over by the Anglican rector. In the atmosphere of the occasion, time stood still, the sermon, preached by the Methodist minister, referred to the prayers which had been etched into the ancient walls of St Mary's. The liturgy took a simple style, with the minimum of ceremonial, and the use of some experimental texts – just to add to the unique character of the occasion. As we prayed, heard the Word read and preached upon, and shared the bread and wine of holy communion, we all had a profound sense of offering the conflict and division of the human race back to God in penitence and hope. Such a sense is not easy to put into words, not least because the churches so quickly united promptly dispersed into separateness, and the war did happen, after all.

But here, nonetheless, was one example of the eucharist emerging from the protective ghetto to which the contemporary Church all too often consigns it, and taking on a new kind of life, its own life, judging the world – and pointing us all to the mercy-seat of God himself.

5

Access to the Word

Part 1

At the beginning of this book we identified the difficulty of managing the crucial one hour or so on Sunday morning. If this is the only time in the week that the parish gathers together, the time is very precious. For those who organize worship the temptation will always be to overfill this time. This will inevitably detract from the essential purpose of Christians drawing together in the presence of God. We all need leisured time for preparation if we are going to bring to God the deeper parts of our lives and allow God to refresh us at our core. Yet if the time on Sunday morning is to be the focus of parish life, all that happens elsewhere in the week will be crying out for some kind of representation. The value of a weekly home prayer group is acknowledged by the time of intercessory prayer in the eucharist. The task of Bible study groups is affirmed by the attention given to Scripture in the sermon. Even the thankless work of a social committee is given due regard by the notices which seem to be an inescapable part of any church service.

Organizers of parish worship are constrained in so many ways. One reaction to this is to reject the constraints by allowing this main act of worship to flow on and on. There are many examples of parish communions lasting two hours or more. However, it is difficult to do this if we are taking seriously the parish as a gathering together of all ages and conditions of men and women. I doubt that many Sunday School helpers can be expected to teach, or crèche helpers expected to look after, children for that length of time. Many people will have other family and social responsibilities that rightly mean that the time dedicated to worship must be kept in proportion. This has important implications for what can then happen within the act of worship.

When I began my appointment as parish priest I inherited a monthly family service which was always a eucharist. However, once a quarter we also welcomed all the Guides, Scouts, Brownies and Cubs. The practice had been to offer a blessing at the altar rail to each child and to all those not yet confirmed. This meant 150 extra heads to bless, which took more than fifteen minutes of the precious time. It was also necessary to finish this service within one hour because the presence of many younger brothers and sisters had been rightly encouraged. I found that once the essential parts of the service had been added, I was left with about three and a half minutes for the readings and address.

A different approach was adopted in a nearby parish. Working with the same range of people, including a predominance of children, they organized an informal Ministry of the Word. Within their church building they could split into smaller groups for teaching and learning. Prayers were led in those groups and also brought into the main gathering. This part of the service was closed with the Peace and coffee in the hall. After twenty minutes those who wanted to receive communion were invited back into the church and quickly taken through a compact version of the Ministry of the Sacrament from Rite A. In these two examples the constraints of congregational practice led either to a shrivelling of the Ministry of the Sacrament or to a non-existent Ministry of the Word. Neither pattern was sustainable and both have now been radically reformed.

The integrity of eucharistic worship requires more than the use of the essential elements. There must be a proper balance, especially between the Word and the Sacrament. If either part is given too little attention, the eucharist as a whole will suffer and die.

This balance can best be achieved by keeping in mind the similar nature of the Ministries of the Word and of the Sacrament. So we have already noted the narrative structure of the eucharistic prayer. This tells us the story of God that is both universal in scope yet particular in detail. The story moves from creation through to the consummation of all things, symbolized by eternal life with God in heaven. Yet in the middle there is the very loaded phrase, 'who in the same night that he was betrayed'. This locates the turning-point of the whole story in the man Jesus and, specifically, in the events of Maundy Thursday and Good Friday. This reminds us that the general notion of God's love is made real in the sacrifice of Christ on the cross. The reality is made present to us in the particular elements of bread and wine that we receive in the eucharist. Whereas many find inspiring the Quaker belief that all the world is a sacrament of God, there is still value in affirming the particularity of God's presence in this part of creation, this bread and this wine.

In the same way, the Ministry of the Word makes God's truth present to us both in overarching and in particular ways. For this part of the service, the particular is much more evident. We only use short readings from the Bible that are clearly part of a larger whole. We bring to God in prayer our special concerns in the intercessions. We are likely to confess to God our own shortcomings and failures in the confession. But the Ministry of the Word is not to be used merely in a limited way, and the whole eucharist will be enriched if this time is seen not just as a personal reflection on Scripture and space for personal prayers. Thus the fullness of God's truth is made present through following a lectionary. This symbolically affirms that all the Bible has a proper place in worship even if a Sunday lectionary cannot literally cover all the text. A set form of intercessions is intentionally composed to represent the needs of the world before God, even if certain parts are more evocative for the individual who prays. One of the great early abbots commended his brothers to confess the sins of the world if they had run out of failures of their own to confess. This presentation of God's truth that takes us beyond particular concerns is formalized in the rubric requiring the Nicene Creed to be said on Sundays and at festivals. What matters is that the whole creed is said by the gathered congregation, thus expressing the faith of the Church. This takes us beyond the question of whether one individual believes each separate item of the creed. It challenges the criterion often heard from hard-pressed leaders of worship: 'We don't say the creed here because it seems unsuited to our needs.'

I would not wish to limit the power of the eucharist by saying that each part must have the same style. For, some people draw closer to God through symbol and image. For these the mystery and majesty of God are especially present in the Ministry of the Sacrament. This part is largely led by the president and the lack of verbal participation by the laity actually enables a closer approach to God. For others, the opposite is true, for it is in speaking to God and in hearing God's Word that they are drawn into God's presence. The Ministry of the Word for them is a time of clarity and enlightenment that reveals God's truth. The integrity of the eucharist is in this regard maintained by the proper *counter-balance* of mystery and clarity, of hiddenness and revelation.

There are important consequences for the way we use the Bible and for preaching in the context of the eucharist.

The narrative structure of the eucharistic prayer is best affirmed by biblical readings that also take the form of a story. This is usually the case for the gospel reading. Many Old Testament texts have a story form, although the narrative is often too extended to include the whole story. An imaginative approach would be for the reader to recount parts of the story in an idiomatic way before reading some of it directly from the text. The epistles apparently do not fit this pattern. Yet many of them clearly are part of a larger story which lies outside the text. For example, some of the most moving and passionate parts of 2 Corinthians make more sense when the dramatic turn-around in relationship between Paul and the Corinthians is understood. This is referred to elsewhere in 2 Corinthians but not in a form that is easily recognized. Some years ago we began in parish worship the practice of introducing the reading from an epistle with a synopsis of the dramatic context. However, it soon became clear that this was a very difficult task, mainly because it was easy to encroach on the work of the sermon. If the role of the reading is one of standing alone, having worth merely because it comes from holy Scripture, then placing the reading in context not only must happen, but also must happen within the sermon.

Another consequence for eucharistic preaching flows from the emphasis on narrative. This preaching must respect the movement of the story. For example, it acknowledges that a parable is not merely a story with a message or a long-winded way of making a point. Rather, meaning is found in the interaction of characters and events and will be unfolded as the sermon progresses. Such preaching cannot easily be summarized in three points and sits ill with the 'Sunday themes' listed in the ASB. Proper respect for the Bible is given when the form of the text influences not only the content but also the nature of the sermon.

Many people have experienced God addressing them directly through the words of Scripture. This happens in a way that does not depend on the original context of the words. This does not contradict what I have said above but is rather an example of God's truth spoken at a particular time for a particular audience. Our use of the Bible and preaching in the eucharist must include this element of direct address. Lectionaries can be overridden for a definite word of challenge or encouragement to be laid before a congregation. There are two classic biblical examples of this. After King David had disposed of Uriah the Hittite so that he could take Bathsheba for himself, Nathan the prophet was sent by God to prophesy against David (2 Samuel 12). Nathan told a story about a rich man, who had many flocks and herds, and a poor man who had only one lamb. When the rich man had to prepare a supper for a visitor, unwilling to take from his own flock, he took the poor man's lamb. This story evoked David's anger and condemnation of the rich man, but Nathan turned David's words on himself as he identified David as the culprit in real life: 'You are the man!' Nathan used the story not to trap David but to evoke in him the proper response that he would not have otherwise given. Such stories involve us fully and when used in preaching will bring into worship the feelings that rightly belong there. A sensitive preacher and leader of worship will choose readings that not only condemn, identifying faults, but also encourage.

This happens in Paul's own use of Scripture in 2 Corinthians 6.2. Quoting from Isaiah, chapter 49, he reminds his hearers about the general truth of God graciously listening to us and helping us. But the word of God is spoken in particular times as well. So Paul declares: '*Now* is the acceptable time. *Now* is the day of Salvation.' These passages clearly identify the action of God's grace in our midst. Therefore it is right, especially in the context of eucharistic worship, that we hear the Now of God clearly spoken. Preaching is not only *about* us, it is directed *to* us.

We have seen that there is another way that the Ministry of the Sacrament can combine the general and the particular. That is by telling the universal story of God's love in a language and style that resonates with our own human predicament. We know that holy communion is a place of God's interaction with us and is not merely a declaration of God's transcendent mystery. For the Ministry of the Word to pick this theme up as well, the Bible must be used in a way that conveys that God listens to us as well as addresses us.

A useful way to approach this has been provided by the Old Testament scholar John Barton. He emphasizes that the primary revelation of God is not the Bible but rather the person of Christ. Therefore, what we have in the Bible, especially in the New Testament, can be described as human reaction to revelation. We have in the epistles the story of how the earliest Christians struggled to find the right way to follow Christ. We have in the gospels not an immediate account of what Jesus did day-by-day in his ministry, but a carefully prepared presentation of who Jesus was and what he did. This was written years after Jesus' resurrection, not merely in order to tell us facts, but, as the gospel of John states, 'that you may believe Jesus is the Christ, the Son of God and that believing you may have life in his name' (John 20.31). So the main texts of the New Testament are records of the early communities of the Christian Church living a life that is a response to the God who revealed himself in the earthly presence of Jesus. When we read these texts now, we can not only draw closer to that primary revelation of God which is Christ, but also we can learn how others based their lives on this revelation.

The words of 2 Timothy 3.16 are often quoted as words of self-authentication: 'All scripture is inspired by God and profitable for teaching, for reproof, for correction, and for training in righteousness.' The Bible is indeed profitable for teaching and training because it records the growth in discipleship of those who follow Christ. We can read evidence of God's grace working in the sinful, arrogant, outspoken and all-too-human lives of the Corinthians. We can be encouraged by the joy and perseverance of the Philippians. When we look carefully at the gospels we can see that Matthew, for example, found in Christ the answers to the problems that were facing his community. This community of Jewish Christians was troubled by pressure from Gentile Christians to abandon their spiritual roots. They were also being challenged by fellow Jews that the vigour and discipline of their religious lives was compromised by Gentile Christians not having to 'fulfil the law'. Matthew's gospel not only presents the story of Christ but does so in a way that these concerns are heard and woven into the story. The communities of Mark and Luke found themselves in very different contexts, and therefore we have the different versions of the story of Christ. The unity of the gospel and the variety of the gospels implies that God will respond to what puzzles and troubles us in our generation also through the story of Christ. As we read the Bible and reflect on it we find that God is listening to us as well as leading us on. This is part of what is meant when we affirm that Scripture is indeed inspired by God.

This means that eucharistic preaching must address itself to the practical and intellectual questions of the listeners. The context of worship is exactly the right place for moral questions or problems of textual criticism to be raised. Advice used to be given that preaching within the eucharist should only address itself to doctrinal or spiritual matters for fear that the emotions or intellect would be too much engaged and so take the listener away from worship. We assert the contrary. My experience has been that a sermon which explored the various contexts of the parable of the Labourers in the Vineyard by means of careful textual criticism led the worshippers into a deeper sense of God's generous grace given here and now. A proper sense of balance will avoid any sermon being based on historical textual questions. But avoidance of this area totally will undermine a sense of God listening to our concerns and so distort our worship.

We need to pursue a little further the idea that God's revelation contains within itself care for the one receiving the revelation. God does not impose his truth on us but presents it in a way that is appropriate for the listener. Indeed, when God's truth is taken into human lives there is always space for a response. There is no virtue in merely speaking the Word if it can neither be heard nor responded to. So I want to question the validity of two types of preaching *within the eucharist*. The first is that which offers verse-by-verse exposition of a text. This style may greatly affirm the importance of and respect for the text, but it excludes response. Even if the preacher raises his or her nose from the text and addresses the matter of application, the style betrays a lack of interest in the particular response offered by the worshippers. They will become numbed, especially if the sermon is followed by reciting the creed, because the personal side of worship will have been excluded for too long. The second type is what is often called 'good solid teaching'. This refers to 30 minutes of careful explanation of some scriptural truth. The implication is that a sermon by its very length becomes good and solid. I do not consider the word 'solid' to fit well in the context of the eucharist. This form of worship is too full of movement, mystery and variation to be called solid. Now, it is clear that at other times in parish life careful study of a text or rigorous teaching on doctrine is right. But sensitivity is needed to discern the ways the Bible can be used in the eucharist and to match the preaching to these ways.

Before we leave this, we must recall the sense that the Ministry of the Word counter-balances the Ministry of the Sacrament and learn from that. Various stories in the Bible refer to both the hiddenness and the revealed nature of God. Perhaps the best known, because it is referred to in the last verse of the hymn 'Dear Lord and Father of mankind', is the story of Elijah in 1 Kings, chapter 19. Although verse 11 states 'the Lord passed by', this is balanced by the words 'but the Lord was not in the wind'. After each awesome manifestation – wind, earthquake and fire – the refrain is heard, 'but the Lord was not in this'. The story is grounded in the hiddenness of God. But the turning-point comes in verse 12, 'and after the fire, a still small voice'. Whereas many sermons have been preached on God revealing himself to us within a still small voice, that is not in the text. The implication is that Elijah at last meets with God, but the balance is very fine. The story does not replace hiddenness with revelation; rather it holds them both together.

In this way, the movement, mystery and narrative that we find especially in the Ministry of the Sacrament is not enough on its own. As humans in relationship with God we need and deserve some clarity as well – the sort of clarity that does not explain away mystery. St Anselm coined the phrase that has been used as the classic way of holding these two parts together: faith seeking understanding. Faith is where we begin, believing on trust at times without experience or knowledge that is our own. Yet within that faith there is a desire to approach the object of faith: God. Faith seeks clarity and understanding so that the faith itself can be strengthened and deepened. Nowadays faith and understanding are frequently described as opposed to one another, but this is not so. As Richard Southern says in his biography of Anselm, 'Reason then may be seen as the appropriate activity for clarifying the contents of faith, just as arranging the contents of a house is the appropriate activity for turning a heap of impedimenta into furnished rooms'. We can be more faithful to God and God can be more active in our lives if there is a cleared space in our hearts and minds.

So eucharistic preaching bears the responsibility for bringing a proper clarity to the community of faith. It will unfold, expand and present what is already believed. For those who are already familiar with the gospel story this preaching will bring to light deeper truths and make connections between pieces already understood. Moreover, the preaching will draw out the varied significance of the eucharist itself. The community will be familiar with the stories of the Passover, Exodus and Covenant given in the Old Testament; with Jesus eating and drinking with sinners in his life, and sharing a final meal with his friends at his death as told in the New Testament; and with prophecies in both Old and New Testaments of the glorious presence of God with his people at a final banquet. But this familiarity needs to be developed into a greater understanding of how these stories can relate to one another. The more we understand through preaching about, say, God's provision of manna in the Exodus, the more we will be able to draw on the stories of Jesus giving himself in his sharing common needs with the outcast. Each aspect of eucharistic truth will illuminate another. As that happens so we will find greater nourishment in our own reception of the sacrament today. Preaching cannot replace God's presence to us in the sacrament but it can make that presence more apparent.

In the resurrection story of the disciples on the road to Emmaus, we find the themes of this chapter movingly presented and united. Two motifs which run through this story are recognition and scriptural interpretation. Yet half the story describes the situation before recognition happens. This gives due weight to the questions and ignorance of the disciples and that, with patience and kindness, Jesus draws near to them and listens. It seems that the disciples have all the pieces that are needed to form faith but they cannot make the necessary connections. They do not recognize the pattern of God in what they already know. The crux of the story comes in Jesus' response. He challenges them in passionate words, referring them to the Scriptures that they should have known. Then he makes the interpretation plain, bringing order to their partial understanding. Jesus is present as the one who listens, addresses and clarifies.

All this is raised to a higher level as they come to the evening meal. With clear reference to the eucharist, Jesus' presence is made fully evident in the breaking of bread. The moment of recognition is also the moment of disappearance. Yet the disciples are left with the powerful feeling that retrospectively Jesus is known in his conversation and in his opening the Scriptures. Word and sacrament are complementary and in balance. The breaking of bread is the occasion of recognition and instrumental in making God's revelation apparent.

Part 2

Symbolism

When I was a boy, we lived in a Scottish village where there was no Episcopal church. This meant that, from time to time, we used to attend the local Kirk. We didn't go just because of the occasional impracticalities of driving to the nearby town for our own service: we didn't want to appear withdrawn from village life. The Presbyterian services were obviously different from what we were used to. But I am glad my parents had a good try at inculcating in me a sense of respect for traditions other than our own.

There was much that was very different. The communion table was in the centre in front of us; behind it was the pulpit. And it was from the pulpit that the morning service was conducted, the minister going down to the table rarely, which made its own impact, for communion was celebrated in those days only four times a year. The service always began in the same way. Before the minister entered and walked up the steps of the pulpit, the beadle (church caretaker) walked in, carrying a large Bible, which he placed on the pulpit reading-desk taking care to unfurl the book-markers, which indicated the two places from which the minister was going to read the lessons, and about which he would – invariably – preach the sermon. Only after the beadle had descended the steps and walked to his place among the congregation did the minister finally enter, in his black silk cassock and gown, academic hood and preaching scarf. It was an impressive sight, so different from the Anglican procession of choirboys, lay reader, and rector, in the other place. It focused the start of the service on the Word of God, read and preached and prayed upon.

Then some years later, I attended my first celebration of the Greek Orthodox liturgy. Again, there was much that was strange. Everyone, except the very elderly and infirm, stood throughout the service. There was no organ droning away in the background, though the chant was traditional Greek, with the droning bass notes speaking through the overlay of upper melody. The air was thick with pungent incense, and everyone in the sanctuary seemed to have a beard. Icons were everywhere, and they kept catching my eye. After the service had been going on for a while (but I soon got used to the idea of time being quite flexible in this eternal-feeling milieu for worship!) one of the doors in the great screen ('iconostasis' or icon-stand) opened, and out walked a deacon, carrying a large and elaborately bound book. He did not just carry it as if it were an ordinary book. He held it high, for all to see. And see we all did – the gold and other precious metals shining out. Accompanied by acolytes with candles and other ministers, he proceeded into the nave and then walked in, with the priest behind him, to the sanctuary, through the central door of the great screen.

It was not until I had studied the Byzantine liturgy in some detail that I eventually learnt that this little ceremony was in origin the start of the eucharist, and what had taken place before that was an office of preparation which the passing of the years had assimilated into the liturgy. But even allowing for that information, I couldn't fail to be impressed by what I saw, and remembered. Here was the Book of the Gospels being brought solemnly into church with all the dignity that could be mustered. And I thought back to the local Kirk, and to the beadle doing the same with the Bible. One sometimes has to have a sense of humour in liturgy, for the two traditions, culturally so far apart, were making exactly the same point: the Bible is the sacred book of the community. Its sacredness is its context.

Context, of course, varies, and it may be suggested that in a technological age such a treatment of the Bible could have no impact whatever. The Orthodox practice of carrying in the Book of the Gospels goes back to the time when books were rare and hand-produced, each page elaborately written by a scribe, and every congregation treasuring its service books in consequence. The Kirk's practice dates from a later century, when, after the invention of printing, the Bible is available for all who can read – and in Reformation Scotland, the grammar schools in the burghs were already making a considerable impact on local literacy. One could say, too, that both such books were the result of a technology, in one case the writing of a liturgical book by hand, in the other case, the printing of a book by machine. Even allowing for the fact that in both congregations there might today be people who could follow the Scriptures with their own Bibles (though I suspect that will be more general in the case of the Kirk than in Orthodoxy), the ceremonial of such treatment at the start of the liturgy nonetheless provides a focus, as well as a sense that the Word of God requires a response, what has been described to me as 'the sacrifice of attention'.

The sacrifice of attention

We have become far too cerebral in our worship these days. Many reasons can be offered: the limitations of time, the effect of the media on the public consciousness, the reluctance to 'come back for more' if the meaning of things doesn't leap at once to one's understanding. The result is that Bible readings – and a lot of preaching – have been deprived of much of their symbolic inner life. The revolution in liturgical texts and the production of too many new versions of the Bible have not helped either, because when worship is destabilized congregations can become disorientated, and they start thinking more about getting their bit 'right' than actually worshipping. New patterns of reading the Bible may throw up a plethora of lesson-readers, many of them on rotas and keen to do their job properly.

It is into this world that the 'sacrifice of attention' is brought to birth. And there is no way of harking back to a past age with ready-made answers. But there are some issues to combat strategically. I sense that the 'cerebral' approach is one of them, and I wonder if the answer now is to concentrate more on the symbol of the word read and preached than on the content. For the greatest symbol in the Christian faith is the cross, not the facts of the cross, nor the circumstances of it, nor even who was to blame. The symbol is the cross itself, which has inspired countless hymn-writers and poets across the centuries. Other symbols abound – the empty tomb of Easter, the foot-washing at the Last Supper, the palm procession – going right back through Jesus' life and ministry to the crib of Bethlehem. A symbol speaks its own language, of which words are but a part, a vehicle, but never the substance. So I lament that many of our old brass lecterns in the form of the eagle (symbol of far-sightedness and heavenly flight) are being discarded in favour of little music stands or slick executive presentation units. The Church can have more confidence in a selective use of its own cultural tradition, as the means of expressing its own language, spoken not in a soliloquy but in dialogue with every age we happen to live in.

An example of such a use of tradition is the icon. Long regarded as something foreign and distant from the West, it has taken on a new lease of life, thanks to the popularity, for example, of Rublev's icon of the Old Testament Trinity. When we were reordering the interior of Holy Trinity, Guildford, we placed the large alabaster font against the south wall of the nave, there being no alternative position, thanks to the west gallery and other constraints. But it became obvious that the font needed a 'backdrop' of some kind, especially in an eighteenth-century interior already full of memorials on the walls. After some consultation, we hit on the idea of a large icon of the baptism of Christ – which would not only point to the font, but also to the Trinity, for the baptism of Christ depicts the Father in the voice, the Spirit in the dove, and the Son in the water. We would therefore be able to have an icon that expressed the dedication of the Church as well. In due time, the icon made its appearance, and it has stirred up a great deal of interest. People regularly pray before it, believing that an icon is no more or less than a picture of someone we love. Above all, the icon has brought alive the narrative power of the baptism of Christ, particularly in the Lucan version, where Jesus *prays* (Luke 3.21, 22).

When it comes to public liturgy, however, there is one question pressing on congregations today – the relationship between Word and Sacrament. For many years, we have been told by our liturgical scholars that there are two parts to the eucharist, which focus round the two symbolic centres of the lectern/pulpit and the holy table. Many of the new liturgies make this abundantly clear in the lay-out of the service books, aided by numbered sections, like the agendas of public meetings. But I suspect that we have gone too far along that road, and I doubt if there is real evidence that the earliest Christian eucharists were sliced up into two parts in quite such a neat manner.

To take what may be the earliest recorded example of all, the walk to Emmaus (Luke 24.13ff.), we can see two interconnected features that could be recovered and reappropriated to advantage in much contemporary worship. One is the context of Jesus listening to our story, and filling in the details only after that listening. The 'sacrifice of attention' is first and foremost God's attention to us, not some superhuman effort of will by human beings to work hard and somehow to get there. The other is the way in which the walk to Emmaus flows into the meal, the walk and the meal being inseparable, not two episodes that somehow have to be cobbled together. Indeed, the walk would be meaningless without Jesus tarrying for the meal, and the meal would have no life of its own without the walk. Perhaps, too, that 'walk' indicates a sense in which contemporary worship needs new ways of beginning, drawing the community gradually towards God, rather than moving angularly and awkwardly through self-conscious bursts of praise and penitence.

How to select from the Bible

What about the way in which the Bible is read? We have stressed the symbolic context. To read the Bible in the Christian assembly is, above all, an activity of the imagination, not a lecture imparting information. But how do the passages get selected? This is a matter that is never finally settled and unfortunately there are a number of rival reading schemes on offer. Two in particular have different backgrounds and it is worth explaining them because they have a particular bearing on worldwide English-speaking Christianity and also because they raise issues about that selection process.

On the one hand, there is the lectionary produced by the British (ecumenical) Joint Liturgical Group in 1967, and which was adopted – with some changes here and there – by the service books of the mainstream Churches of the British Isles, except the Roman Catholic Church. This lectionary works on a two-year cycle, and although the official version carefully avoids the term, it is in fact broadly 'thematic' in its approach to Scripture. At first sight, this seems sensible, particularly at festivals, when the readings need to harmonize, because if you are celebrating Easter, you want to have lections that fit together around that central truth. But it does not sit easily with a Sunday at the back-end of August! This is where most difficulty has been encountered. And, in retrospect, one can see how the 'biblical theology' movement that was fashionable among scholars after the Second World War has influenced this particular lectionary. 'Biblical theology' was at root an attempt to harmonize the books of the Bible together, to make them relate to each other, and proclaim certain truths with a common mind. But all movements can be taken too far. The Joint Liturgical Group lectionary was, for example, incorporated into the Alternative Service Book of the Church of England. There is growing dissatisfaction with its contents because the readings are long (which is why most congregations leave out the Old Testament or the epistle reading in spite of recommendations to the contrary).

The other lectionary began its life in the Roman Catholic Church after the Second Vatican Council, when, after centuries of using the same readings, it was decided to open up the Scriptures to worshippers in a way that would have been thought impossible centuries before. The group charged with the task of producing this scheme looked at as many lectionaries as possible, and also had the courtesy to consult with other Christian Churches to see what they were doing. In the end, a three-year lectionary was produced, in which each of the first three gospel-writers would figure prominently in one year, and John's gospel would be used at solemn and festal seasons (according to tradition), and also fill in during the comparatively thin year of Mark's gospel. Moreover, unlike the Joint Liturgical Group scheme, which hops around from one gospel to another, this new scheme reads gospels and epistles in a serial form, so that congregations get the chance to gain a sense of continuity from one Sunday to another.

This lectionary was adopted, with some adaptation, by other Churches in North America, and increasingly throughout the English-speaking world. Indeed, there was a time when some countries which had gone for the British Joint Liturgical Group's scheme then discarded it in favour of the Roman Catholic one. That is where we are in the British Isles today, and it is likely that the international 'ecumenical' version of the

Roman lectionary (called the 'Revised Common Lectionary') will be included in the revision of the Alternative Service Book in due course.

All this sounds somewhat distanced from the ordinary life of a parish. Decisions about what is to be read are not just a matter of personal whim. There will be occasion: when whatever central authority directs will be discarded. But congregations need a sense of security. It is likely that the three-year lectionary will become the major international scheme among those Churches which use a formal liturgy for some time to come. It is not a perfect scheme – but no lectionary is. For example, it is still not clear how the Old Testament should be read in 'ordinary time' (the 'green Sundays'). The original Roman Catholic version selected these from here and there in order to give a good flavour of the various books in question, whereas there have been proposals recently to try to read some of the Old Testament books in some kind of 'serial' form, which is not always easy.

In all this time of experimentation, it can seem a tall order to inculcate a sense among worshippers that we are, indeed, taking part in an activity of the imagination. Those who read the Scriptures at the public assembly – clerical and lay – need to spend far more time looking not only at what they have to read, but also at the other readings on the occasion, and the readings that came on the previous Sunday as well as the Sunday following! They need, too, to have far greater confidence that they are not going to say it all, for the Scriptures are really less like reading a 'lesson' than like playing a piece of music from a score. Let me give a ready example.

In the church where I habitually worshipped, we were using the Revised Common Lectionary, which brought a great liberation to many people, the preachers included, for it is more demanding to preach on the gospel Sunday by Sunday if it is the same gospel-writer week after week than if one is moving constantly around from one to another. The preacher normally reads the gospel, which provides a focus and a dramatic context. At the morning prayer that precedes the eucharist, which is attended by the clergy, chalice ministers, lesson-readers, and other lay assistants, we normally have only one lesson; sometimes this is the gospel for the day. On one occasion, the person asked to read it at morning prayer remarked at the end of the eucharist how totally differently I had read it in the eucharist, and how interesting that was. We then went straight into a conversation about the unsearchable riches of the Scriptures. And my mind went back to the way in which the minister of the Kirk used to conclude each reading in the morning service: 'And may God add unto us His blessing from the reading of His most holy Word, and to His name be the glory and the praise. Amen.' Is this more dramatic – if a bit ponderous – in comparison with 'This is the Word of the Lord – Thanks be to God'? At least it points to the *reading* of the Word of God. (Some modern liturgies leave out the aggressively demonstrative 'This is' and rest content with 'The Word of the Lord'.) But whatever the content of the liturgical formula, to read the Scriptures at public worship is nothing less than co-operating with God, 'actualizing' his loving purpose, his constant conversation with people down through history up into eternity.

Pressures on the sermon

I feel much more sorry for preachers today than I would have a hundred years ago! Whereas in bygone years, the sermon was for many people one of their only experiences of public discourse, nowadays the sermon has to compete with the highly professionalized media experts, who are many of them trained to a peak of talent in using just the right word here, the pause for breath there, and the correct length of sentence to make the right point. Not that they are all fine performers. Sometimes one can get a little tired of short and pithy sentences, containing too much information and analysis and therefore lacking colour and variety. Augustine wrote some quite lengthy sentences, where he sometimes appears to get a little lost, but his one-liners are always worth waiting for, like this repeated prayer to God in Book X of *Confessions,* where he breaks through his soul-searching on the power and complexity of memory with the words 'Grant what you command and command what you will'.

It is not just style that puts pressure on the sermon – but also length. I was told when I was a student 'to preach about God and about ten minutes'. But I know people who have consistently criticized the Church for giving in to this common attitude because they have left the church building on a Sunday morning ill served by a few pious thoughts from the chancel step.

Augustine's prayer to God to fulfil his promises makes a significant statement about the fact that God's promises are eternal, and yet we have to grapple with them in our own time and in our own civilization. It is a fallacy to assume that the sermon was a remote, impersonal, unchanging activity until someone invented the radio and then the television. Sermons have long varied. It is interesting to observe, for example, how the famous diarist John Evelyn, who lived a generation after Lancelot Andrewes in the later seventeenth century, disliked the sermons he heard which self-consciously imitated the Andrewes style. He was no longer in fashion.

The sermon, however, has one main advantage, way above the radio or the television, and that is that it is preached *live.* There is nothing quite like being present on the occasion, being in the congregation, at the eucharist, with the people, who have heard a particular sermon, even if it wasn't quite as slick or professionally delivered as it might have been if broadcast. Even so, congregations can get bored with the slick, well-staged performances in which nothing goes wrong, just as they can get irritated when they witness a shambles every week and no one – least of all the preacher – appears to care.

For preaching is first and last a conversation. It is not a discourse held 'out there' for people to 'listen to' and that is that. Congregations like to get to know their preachers, and the cumulative effect of a good, unpretentious preacher on the eucharistic assembly over the years cannot be underestimated.

Much that is intangible is inevitably communicated. A way of life is proclaimed. Self-importance is redressed. Bad habits – yes, the pulpit isn't all reassurance and comfort – identified. The heart of the matter of preaching is for the preacher's understanding of God and of the human race to come through, especially how God and humanity meet and converse.

This means that congregations can help preachers by being more conscious of the different strands that make up a sermon, or, better still, the different kinds of sermon that are preached. I have seldom felt constrained by thirteen minutes at a sung eucharist when I have wanted to blend in something about the readings, something about where the people might be, some-thing about their devotional lives, and something about where the sacrament fits into all of this. It may seem a tall order, and there are times when it is necessary to cast this aside and opt for only one strand. Moreover, I wonder if preachers nowadays have lost interest in heaven. Lancelot Andrewes repeatedly ended his sermons either with a call to come forward for communion, or with a joyous celebration of the life of heaven that awaits – and he frequently did both. The union of the earthly and the heavenly is not just about singing the Sanctus in the eucharistic prayer. Preaching is about the kingdom, and if that kingdom is limited to the here and now, all it will do is leave the congregation with a sense of frustration: 'We won't manage *all* of this by next week.' It is quite possible to preach about heavenly virtues in such a way as to challenge the hearers with a message for now and also beckon them to the end of all things.

There are many jokes about sermons, not just about their length. And there are preachers who attempt to get the atten-tion of the congregation with a nice little run-in story. It is often a good technique, but it can also at times be discarded to advantage. What people need in preaching is to be *fed*. Nothing forced or contrived will do this. But a congregation appreciates a preacher who has thought and prayed hard about their lives – not just their sufferings (and they can be real) but also their accomplishments. The gospel is not just about comfort: it is about joy.

One of the best preachers I heard as a boy was James Stewart, who after many years in parish ministry became a Professor at New College, Edinburgh. He had the knack of preaching with passion and realism that few could aspire to, and yet he was in personal terms a modest, quiet man, with a deep love of life and people. There was always a sense of urgency about his preaching, a fearlessness that the things of God *mattered*. He had confidence in the message, but knew there would be times when the church would be cold, the congregation thin and the preacher bereft of a startling message to liven everything up. Those low, routine points are precious moments in the life of faith, for we cannot always live on a high. There are, to put it bluntly, many news bulletins that are limited in content; there are glossy films that say nothing new; and newspapers are, after all, mostly *daily*, here today and gone tomorrow.

But the preacher has a duty above all this, and so does the congregation. How many people pray for their preachers as they mount the steps of the pulpit to deliver something deep in their hearts? How many communicants wait to be fed from the preacher as if this were no mere prelude to the eucharistic bread and wine but part of the divine feeding? At the end of a series of lectures to aspiring ministers of the Kirk, subsequently published as a bestseller, *Heralds of God*, Stewart speaks from the heart:

> I pray that God will mightily bless your ministry. May He fulfil and verify in your experience those words which stand in the enactments of Leviticus, but which must surely mean far more for you to-day than the writer of any code in Israel could ever comprehend: 'The Fire shall ever be burning upon the altar; it shall never go out.'

6

c/se/se/s

Access to communion

Part 1

On the day I took up my first post as vicar of a parish, I was greeted in the street by a smart, rather reserved, middle-aged woman. 'It's so nice', she said, 'to have a young vicar again. Perhaps you will get rid of all this handshaking nonsense.' She was referring to the greeting of Peace offered to fellow worshippers in the middle of the communion service. This act had become for her, as for many others, an embarrassing and false expression of sentiment in the middle of a deeply personal period of worship. She felt forced to participate in a time of genial bonhomie which she considered to be inappropriate and exclusive. For her, this 'nice young vicar' was the man to stamp out such nonsense. I was puzzled by this, for it is often the younger generation that has been accused of introducing more informality and feeling into the set patterns of worship. Then I realized that she saw the new vicar as the one to sweep away the accretions of the progressive 1970s and 1980s and return the parish to a purer form of worship.

In a way, I was content with that role, for I had long felt that 'the Peace' had been hijacked by one particular way of sharing the Peace. I remember the time some years ago when offering a handshake at the Peace was reintroduced to the parish where I grew up. Then the Vicar explained that it was a very ancient custom. In times of persecution, it was dangerous to meet together for Christian worship. For the first part of the service, baptized, committed believers and enquirers would share a time of prayer and learning from the Scriptures. But there came a moment when those who were not fully received into the Christian community were required to leave the building. Only then was it safe to proceed with the breaking of bread. Before that happened, when it was known that only Christians were present, they shared together the Peace – and, I am sure, offered one another the third-century equivalent of the hand-shake. This the Vicar explained and this we began to do with a certain degree of excitement, nervousness and embarrassment. I have seen the same reaction to something new when I have watched a young boy be inducted as a new Scout. He has to learn to do the special salute and Scout handshake. It feels exciting and new, but the boy is warned also to get it right, for he knows that these signs are significant. The salute and hand-shake are many-faceted ritual signs that communicate a good deal both to fellow Scouts and to those on the outside.

However, what has happened in the Church is that, over a period of a few years, the significance of the sign of Peace has shrunk. In practice it is frequently now performed solely to convey messages about the relationship between fellow worshippers. Christians, who know each other well, gather for worship on Sunday and, in the middle of the communion service, hug and kiss each other, clap each other on the back with smiles and laughter. Some will do this in an unashamedly public way feeling that they are fulfilling the verse 'see how these Christians love one another'. The Peace not only has become a time for mutual encouragement amongst believers but also is used as a sign to proclaim what is on offer in ideal Christian relationships.

There are others who stand by, looking on, in embarrassed silence. The embarrassment is different to the feeling we had in the early years. Then we were beginning to do well some-thing that was important and new to us, like the young Boy Scout. Now there are many who enjoy sharing the Peace, but also feel that something has been lost by an over-emphasis on intimate sentiments. The Peace has many layers of meaning, reaching beyond expressing relationships between fellow worshippers. These need to be identified and reaffirmed.

Those years ago, our vicar began his explanation of the Peace with the words 'In times of persecution'. Times are different now for all of us. How we celebrate the Peace and when we do it will depend on how we understand the boundary between the body of worshippers and the outside world. For example, in a suburban town there is no persecution or hostility shown towards a church. Indeed, the general feeling is one of apathy towards the Christian faith. So on Sunday morning as the worshippers gather, there is a lot of chatter before the service begins. People are greeting one another, and telling stories about the past week. Here is a place where you are known by name, whereas outside many feel there is an atmosphere of anonymity. Yet, because there is no hostility shown to Christians, there is no sense of withdrawing from the world; rather, there is a sense of gathering together in a place of comfort and warmth. I know many people who complain of the noise before the service and how difficult it is to begin the 'proper' worship. An alternative approach would be to say that this is the Peace happening informally. So the service could begin in a gradual way with the first greeting from the Vicar being 'The Peace of the Lord be always with you', confirming what has already begun.

In a slightly different context, the Peace realistically happens at the end of the service. In a city parish, people arrive at church rather more guarded and wary of what is happening in the streets outside. They are glad to meet up with fellow believers, but it takes time for them to relax into fellowship and trust. At the end of service, the time spent over coffee is very much appreciated and strengthens everyone for the week ahead. It seems that the Peace is happening at the close of the service. The link between the Peace and the dismissal is already present when the president uses the words 'Go in peace to love and serve the Lord'. It may be right for this also to be the time to share the Peace with an appropriate greeting.

These examples show that, for the Peace to work as an

effective sign, we need to be aware of more than merely the relationship between fellow worshippers. What is being expressed in this sign includes attitudes, conscious or not, about the boundary between worshippers and the world outside. If we continue to consider where else the Peace can happen during the communion service, we will see that different beliefs are also being expressed. These beliefs concern the relationship between the love of our neighbours and the love of God.

So many people complain about the Peace because it occurs in the middle of the communion service just at the point when they are feeling stilled, quiet within themselves and in the presence of God. These people value the Prayer of Humble Access which powerfully focuses their attention on communion with God and their need for being fed by God himself. It is then an enormous transition suddenly to rise from prayer and physically to greet one's neighbour. People resent the Peace because they feel they are being taken out of communion with God.

One response to this begins with the passage in Matthew, chapter 5, which speaks of being reconciled to our brother or sister before approaching the altar. So the Peace is properly placed in the middle of the service exactly before we approach the altar. We may feel that we are moving into deeper communion with God in prayer but, *before* this can happen, we must make peace with our brother or sister. This theological emphasis is that the love of neighbour must come before the love of God.

However, there is another way of relating these two loves. This way is to emphasize that the love of neighbour is part of our loving God, rather than seeing them as two separable loves. It is in the very act of greeting, caring for and respecting our neighbour that we also express our love for God. This is the message that is clearly found in the first epistle of John. The author repeatedly asserts that to love God not only requires us to love our brothers and sisters, but is found in such love. This is expressed liturgically by placing the Peace right next to the act of receiving communion. In the Roman Catholic rite, worshippers offer the Peace not at the beginning of the ministry of the sacrament but immediately before the reception of the sacrament. The two loves could not be more intimately connected; as worshippers are drawn closer to one another, they also draw closer to God. In my personal prayers I find this truth expressed in the final prayer after communion. We say the words 'Almighty God, we thank you for feeding us with the body . . . of Christ'. Clearly the purpose of the prayer is to direct our attention to having received the bread and wine. But I value also the ambiguity which enables me to thank God for having been fed by the body of Christ, that is, the people I have worshipped with. Through the act of coming together with others for worship I am strengthened to live and work to God's praise and glory. I believe that this approach of loving God by loving neighbour forms the basis for many people's daily discipleship.

I have experienced the Peace at yet another place in the communion service, that is, after the sermon and before the intercessions. Significantly this was in a healing service where the laying-on of hands was offered as well as the sacrament of bread and wine. The service broke into three parts, the first being the preparation for worship, readings and sermon. Before moving into the ministry of the sacrament, the third part, there was a time of greeting one another, sharing together topics for prayer, both individual and communal, followed by an extended time of informal intercession. In effect, this part began with the Peace and only when that had happened could we move into prayer. The emphasis here was that we needed to know one another before we could love one another, and that this love was presented to God in the intercessions. The Peace therefore played an important part in the process that moved from being known to being accepted to being loved. That is the pattern that is so often seen in the healing stories in the gospels. Jesus focuses his attention on the person in need, accepts them as they are (often with a word of forgiveness) and finally demonstrates the power of God's love through making the person whole.

So far we have seen how different aspects of the Peace are highlighted by considering the place of this act in the service. Two further aspects come to light as we look at the Peace, first as a sign of the kingdom and then as a specifically ritual act.

The gospels record that Jesus told many parables about the kingdom of God and left many individual sayings about the kingdom. Some stress the presence of the kingdom, really in the world now.

> But if it is by the Spirit of God that I cast out demons, then the kingdom of God has come upon you. (Matthew 12.28)

> And Jesus answered them, 'Go and tell John what you hear and see: the blind receive their sight and the lame walk, lepers are cleansed and the deaf hear, and the dead are raised up, and the poor have good news preached to them.' (Matthew 11.4–5)

> Being asked by the Pharisees when the kingdom of God was coming, he answered them, 'The kingdom of God is not coming with signs to be observed; nor will they say, "Lo, here it is!" or "There!" for behold, the kingdom of God is in the midst of you.' (Luke 17.20–21)

Some stress that the kingdom of God is still to come. We pray for this in the Lord's Prayer (Matthew 6.10). There is the question of who would sit at Jesus' right hand in the coming kingdom (Mark 10.35–45). There is Jesus' saying that he would not drink wine again until he drinks new wine when the kingdom has come (Mark 14.25).

For years scholars have debated which of these sayings are original to Jesus and which may have originated in the early Christian communities. They have disagreed about which group of sayings is more important, and about how the two groups can be united into one consistent whole. Theological fashions change but what is clear is that both groups are part of the biblical tradition and sense can be made of both groups of sayings. Therefore the kingdom of God is properly described both as present now here on earth, and also as still awaited in all its fullness.

Ambiguities that lie within the act of the Peace match the ambiguities that surround the kingdom of God. We must affirm what is already present amongst us and we do so by declaring at the Peace 'we are the body of Christ'. God is active here and now, in and through his people. This is seen as they share a common life that is founded on baptism and is maintained by mutual peace and love. Many people today favour this approach because it is easy to identify who we are at peace with and what this peace means. Hence the emphasis is on the present experience of the feelings of worshippers.

But we must also affirm that what we experience now is not complete and the fullness of God's kingdom and God's peace is still to come. Only when God's rule is fully established and all that opposes God is destroyed will there be true peace. In Isaiah 25.6–8, there is the prophecy that God will swallow up tears and death for ever and that the people will eat together the ultimate banquet in peace. Echoes of this are found in the great prophecy at the end of Revelation (21.1–8), which even more firmly places this event in the future. So those who complain that they do not feel at one with other worshippers, and so refuse to share the Peace, have forgotten this future aspect. We are not invited merely to share what is present; in the Peace we affirm what is to come.

I experienced this in a small way one year when working at a Christian youth camp. On the final evening, there was to be an open-air communion service drawing on the fellowship and teaching of the previous fortnight. Bad feelings had been simmering between myself and Tony, another member of the team, which broke into open hostility just before the service began. As I sang the first hymn I watched this man walking away up the hillside. I felt worried, guilty and totally ill at ease as we approached the Peace. The invitation to show a sign of peace left me cold until I saw Tony approaching me with his hand outstretched. Then I realized that this was indeed a *sign* of peace even if it could not yet be peace itself. This was peace-making, though it took many hours of further talk for us both to find forgiveness.

Indeed, I have always valued that we were somehow forced into this by the liturgy. We were not asked first to come together face to face; rather, we were invited to perform a ritual act. We knew how to do this, we knew what was expected and it was safe. Contrary to common expectations that ritual is insincere and only on the surface, this ritual began something that was real and profound.

So far I have suggested different approaches to the sign of Peace that lead us deeper into its meaning, but in the end I need to suggest that we keep the Peace also as a recognizable, slightly formal ritual performance. Only then will it also be able to deliver the deeper aspects of meaning.

Ritual is valuable because it is reliable. Over some months I used to visit a counsellor. In the consulting room we sat opposite one another with a definite space in between, talking and in silence. Each week when I left the house, we shook each other's hand. When I asked about this one day my counsellor said 'It is not right for us to touch in there, but it is good to do so here'. I appreciated that moment of contact which was reliable and safe. In a similar way some widows have said to me how much they value the Peace because it is the one time in the week that they are hugged. If they were to ask for this at other times, they could be misunderstood. But at the sign of Peace they are in touch with others in a way that is real, safe and profoundly moving. We need therefore to maintain the sign of Peace not as an opportunity for extravagant displays of feeling, but as an occasion when we express many truths about ourselves, our neighbours and our God.

Part 2

Two stories about the Peace

Late in 1959, Angelo Roncalli, the Patriarch of Venice, was elected Pope. As John XXIII, he began a short reign that was to open the door to strong winds of new life into the Roman

Catholic Church – and far beyond. Many are the stories told about him. On being asked how many people worked in the Vatican, he replied 'about half of them'.

However, his official 'coronation' (as it was called in those days) was anything but the result of winds of change. I remember sitting and watching parts of it on television. It seemed to be endless, but, then, I was not entirely familiar with the intricacies of the old Roman Catholic rite. Of course I remember well the moment at which the great three-tiered crown (or 'tiara') was placed on his head. But what stuck in my mind – and I cannot reason why! – was the point in the service when the cardinals and others in the sanctuary greeted each other. I had never seen anything like it before in my life. Cardinal after cardinal – or so it seemed – was escorted to colleagues, to whom each bowed, and then each raised their arms to the other's shoulders, and extended right cheek forward to the left, taking care not to touch the other in any way. After this seemingly meaningless gesture, the bow was repeated and we were off for another such greeting.

Obviously there was some kind of greeting going on. But it was theatrical, it involved nothing tactile and it was confined to certain people in high places in the service. It was not until many years later that I learnt exactly what was going on. It was nothing more or less than the Kiss of Peace, as it had survived in an archaic form in the Roman Pontifical. It had survived as a relic of something past, akin to what the zoologists called 'arrested evolution', when an animal of some sort stops developing because it has no need to, and probably sticks out like a sore thumb when set alongside other more 'modern' living creatures.

Many years later, as a student, I attended a conference on how worship should be taught in colleges. It was a chance for me to get my own back on my teachers and their colleagues! Unfortunately, my rebellion was a non-event, largely because the teachers wanted to do to the syllabus roughly what my generation of students desired. We wanted to set up some kind of dialogue between the tradition as we needed to understand it, and the way people lived and felt today. In the course of one of the plenary sessions, Walter Hollenweger, a well-known writer on the world Church, told the story of an experimental eucharist in a Swiss city, where the congregation of the main Reformed Church were indubitably very Swiss, very tidy and very devout. In and around the centre of the city were coffee houses frequented by those burghers themselves, where the waiters were all Spanish or Italian. The experiment was to relate the Lord's Supper to its actual surroundings. As the congregation entered church, each was offered a cup of hot coffee, freshly brewed, by these waiters. The offertory procession involved bread and wine – and a large pile of coffee beans. And then, as if to cap it all, instead of the congregation's elders serving the bread and wine at communion, the place of the elders was taken by the Spanish and Italian waiters. For just as their role in life was to serve the community with their refreshments, so in the liturgy they were – just for once – to serve them the food and drink of the eucharist.

The result was mixed. Some of those present were furious. Why should they have to hear all these foreign languages in church, when they had to listen to them all the week round? Others confessed to a sense of the real presence of Christ for the first time. One Spanish waiter wrote afterwards 'I thank the Lord for the privilege of celebrating the Lord's Supper with my Swiss brethren'.

Can the Peace have a role – with its history?

The two stories recounted above are both true. But when they are told like that they give the sense of caricature. The old papal coronation, with all its formality and archaic ceremonial, giving the impression of a Church that is uninterested in anything going on around it, contrasts uneasily with the radical, sudden jolt of a Swiss Reformed eucharist at which the world outside is, for once, permitted to get inside, and not only do that, but have an authentic place within the service.

But we cannot survive as a community if we have to live with either of these kinds of events all the time. A church whose liturgy is theatrical all the time becomes the laughing-stock of the rest of civilization. On the other hand, a church which sets out all the time to make bold, radical statements about Life As It Is Really Lived will soon be ignored. So we are back at the heart of the eucharist, and the nature of ritual.

Ritual involves symbolic action: the taking of bread and wine within a particular context. It involves repetition (or rather, 'iteration', as it is often nowadays called), so that the community has a sense of being taken up into that story. It involves a judicious degree of variety, so that the context can be both universal (the work of Christ) and particular (my own needs, please). It involves, too, the risk of not always being understood (Jeremy Taylor's language of mystery). And nowhere is all this truer than when we come to look at the Peace.

It is clear that the first Christians did not regard it as a trivial 'hello'. Some of the New Testament epistles end with the greeting of a holy kiss (2 Corinthians 13.12; 1 Thessalonians 5.26; 1 Peter 5.14), or they refer to greeting or to peace in conclusion (Romans 16.20; 1 Corinthians 16.20; Galatians 6.16; Ephesians 6.23; Philippians 4.21; 2 Thessalonians 3.16). It obviously said something about the nature of Christian fellowship – in one another and the Lord. Peace, after all, in Hebrew 'shalom', is a greeting both intimate and God-centred. It should not surprise us that the first Christians introduced it into the eucharistic liturgy. It tended to appear at the point where, as we now call them, the two parts of the service come together; at the end of the Word and when the table is about to be prepared. It may well be that this position was favoured because of Jesus' words of warning that we should leave our gifts at the altar and first be reconciled with our fellows before making the offering (Matthew 5.24).

But other positions were found. In the Greek Orthodox Church, it is given just before the creed is recited, which comes just before the eucharistic prayer – which may be said to express unity in belief. In the Roman rite, it has come for many centuries just before communion, after the bread has been broken – which may be said to express unity in the broken bread and the communion.

At the Reformation, because the gesture was relatively unknown in any form in ordinary parochial worship, the Peace only survived as a verbal greeting, so that in many places the old words 'The peace of the Lord be always with you' (or their equivalent) were retained. So it was in England in the first Prayer Book (1549). This was changed with the second Prayer Book (1552), the words of the blessing at the end being sufficient, taken from Philippians 4.7: 'The peace of God, which passeth all understanding, keep your hearts and minds in the knowledge and love of God, and of his Son Jesus Christ our Lord . . . '

Research into the origins of Christian worship that has had so great an impact on the compilation of new liturgies this century was bound to unearth the ancient form of this greeting. The first united Church, that of South India, introduced it before the offertory in its innovative communion rite. From there, the custom has spread, surprisingly, into all kinds of cultures where it would once have been shunned. It still causes embarrassment. But my hunch is that, except in those places where it has been allowed to run riot, it will be around for a long time to come.

Like other forms of ritual, the handshake, the hug, the gentle touching of another person, is bound to give different kinds of signals. There is no point telling people exactly what it means. They will make their own meaning. But a little help in its origin and development never goes amiss. Unity, fellowship, welcome, reconciliation, comfort, these are all varieties of the 'shalom' that we are all called to know and share. There have been times when I have greeted a recently widowed person at this point in the service and it has been both deeply moving and very real. As a naturally shy person, I have found getting used to the Peace far more difficult than I have often admitted to others. But the biggest irony about the Peace is the stage in the history of Western culture in which we are now. For at precisely the time when the rest of the world has become increasingly suspicious of the tactile in public – or less private – life, the Church enjoys the freedom of being able to greet its members in an open space, without fear of being accused of insidious motives. That is exactly the kind of counter-cultural message that the Christian community is called upon to proclaim. So, for all the criticisms and strange stories that can be told about this gesture, I for one am keen for it to stay, provided that it doesn't die a death of trivialization.

Peace and communion

One of the important functions that old liturgies can perform for the rest of us is to preserve ancient practices, even if they are concealed under curious clothing. One such is, clearly, the Peace. When I began to get used to shaking hands with people in church, I soon became very thankful that this greeting had been kept alive by part of the wider Church. Ritual is about formality, and it can also know forms of recovery. That much many of us have experienced in recent years, with all the upset and excitement that this can bring with it.

The Peace is a winner for the eucharist, because it has a life that is so close to the meal of the baptized community. Even if we stopped the gesture, we could never leave the reality, the promise, the hope of God's wholeness of life, far outside the eucharistic table. And if we did, we would be turning our backs on something so Christian that we would be in danger of forgetting our vocation altogether. Anything important, of course, can be interpreted broadly. In an earlier chapter, we saw how forgiveness is not confined to the recitation of the absolution – it belongs at the font, at the communion table, at the pulpit, in prayer as well. The presence of Christ, too, is not to be confined to the bread and wine. One needs to start with the general, and from there move into the particular – a good method for dealing with any matter.

The Peace, therefore, is about God, and God's purpose of wholeness not just for us but for the created order. Perhaps we are apt to confine the Peace to the relational and forget that it is also about the world transformed, 'transfigured', by its Lord. Issues of pollution are not just about the wastepaper basket.

They are also about the way we relate to each other and to the world. A renewed created order is one in which we can strive to live a life that is 'whole'. Bread and wine are the result of the dying and the rising of created elements: corn crushed and baked with yeast, grapes crushed and fermented with sugar. The Peace is the result of human beings able to surrender themselves to each other in the unity of God himself. The eucharistic elements and the gesture of Christian greeting are both about life being transformed and transfigured by Christ.

How exactly does this come about? In one way, the answer to that question is 'wait and see'. We do not know the precise mechanisms of the kingdom of God. They are God's secrets. But there is one way in which we can contemplate this mystery, and here the words of the liturgy can, for once, speak with an unambiguous voice.

One of the standard ways of introducing the Peace is:

> We are the Body of Christ.
> In the one Spirit we were all baptized into one body.
> Let us then pursue all that makes for peace
> and builds up our common life.

Then, in the eucharistic prayer, the president always says:

> Take, eat; this is my body which is given for you.

Then, later on, the prayer after communion almost invariably gives thanks:

> Almighty God,
> we thank you for feeding us
> with the body and blood of your Son Jesus Christ.

And, finally, at the very end:

> Go in *peace* to love and serve the Lord.

There is a progression between these various aspects of the eucharist. We are the body, yet this is my body. We give thanks for being fed, yet we are to go in his peace. Sometimes the words of worship have been described as 'assiduous supposing'. Here are words that go beyond the immediately practical, what can be realized in a matter of moments. The words, it has to be said, ask rather more than the literal mind will allow. And then we go out to the banal world we know all too well, perhaps having a cup of coffee on the way, and to catch up with parish gossip, or even speak to a newcomer.

Is this fair, or is it a parody of the eucharist? If these words are to mean anything, can they ever be so misinterpreted?

Parody and misinterpretation result from a determination to see only one side of the question. We warned in an earlier chapter against triumphalism. That doesn't mean apologizing for what we have been given, but it does mean trying to avoid being arrogant about it. The key, it seems to me, lies in the very fragile character of the human being's gesture towards others, which is mirrored in the fact that bread and wine are themselves the fruit of fragility, the dying and rising again of corn and grape. For it is the close identification of Jesus with his followers and the eucharistic elements at the Last Supper that makes it inevitable that the most supreme way in which they would 'remember' him, call to mind his life, his love, his suffering, his triumph, would be to gather round that table time and again, in order to be fed with the food that endures right through to the end.

The earliest Christians were much more conscious of the eucharistic elements as creatures of God, which is vividly portrayed in some of the early liturgies. In recent centuries, there has been much controversy in eucharistic theology, particularly over how Christ is present and how far the service can be called a sacrifice. Contemporary ecumenical agreement tends to see these issues more whole, and to place them in the total picture of God acting through the entire celebration. Presence and sacrifice can be seen in a distorted manner, rather like two great pillars in a landscape that is in fact of greater interest than the pillars themselves.

I wonder whether the kind of deep reflection on the meaning of the Peace and the story of the act of communion itself might not lead to a more wholesome eucharistic scene, in which lifestyle flows from Christ's presence at the meal, a presence itself of self-giving, of sacrifice, of love and forgiveness. Many of the issues that have divided Christians in the past have now faded from the scene, at least as far as most lay people are concerned. Perhaps there is a tendency to underestimate the importance of the differences as they still exist at the official level. And yet these fresh perspectives on the relationship between 'we are the body' and 'this is my body' draw together in a way that would have been unthinkable in the days before the Peace was reintroduced. For here is theology played out in the liturgy. Here is Christian teaching acted out in worship. Here is the essence of the gospel being restored to the eucharist. We do not celebrate the eucharist in order to place all our doctrinal, aesthetic, or even musical goods in the shop window. We celebrate the eucharist in order to grasp a better vision of life with God.

Similarly, in an age in which we are more than ever conscious of the need to see creation as part of our responsibility, it may well be that we begin to look upon the bread and the wine as signs of that new creation which has been promised and of which the eucharist is itself a harbinger. Poor, weak, puny elements, like the baby in the crib at Bethlehem! And the vehicles of God's self-giving love, the seeds of a new world that starts now.

One of the earliest Christian prayers comes from the *Didache*, a book of church life and worship that probably comes from Syria, within the lifetime of the New Testament. It expresses much of what I am trying to say:

> As this broken bread was scattered over the mountains and when brought together became one, so let your Church be brought together from the ends of the earth into your kingdom; for yours are the glory and the power through Jesus Christ for evermore.

7

c/೨e/೨e/೨

Access to the results

Part 1

In the years before the eucharist was widely used as the regular form of parish Sunday worship, I remember being caught up in a fraught discussion. One friend said that she preferred to receive communion at most once or twice a year. This was for her such a special form of worship that she needed time to prepare herself. Participating in a communion service was not to be undertaken lightly and she drew strongly on the words of Paul: 'Whoever, therefore, eats the bread or drinks the cup of the Lord in an unworthy manner will be answerable for the body and blood of the Lord. Examine yourselves, and only then eat of the bread and drink of the cup' (1 Corinthians 11.27–28). Each act of communion for her was a notable and holy occasion. Another friend spoke movingly about his practice of receiving communion on a daily basis. He described the sustenance he received from this as well as the challenge it presented to dedicate each day to God. I was caught in the middle in a naïve way, not realizing that choice was possible. As some parishes are now beginning to feel the constraints of a weekly eucharist, an answer to the question why we repeat the eucharist should help us determine how frequently we wish to repeat it. If the eucharist is a service of remembrance, how often do we need to be reminded of the past?

That is a loaded way of putting the question, for remembering is not just about the past. Human memory does not merely play back events of the past as a tape recorder might, but it is an active function of the brain that involves the whole person. As I remember an event of my childhood, I am drawing on my past and combining it with what I have seen, felt and thought since then. All this is affected too by the sort of person I am now. So, one of my earliest memories is of my brother pushing me against the corner of our house. I can visualize this clearly now and still feel the pain of it. However, I was taken aback when I saw a photograph of our old house and realized that the location was not as I remembered it. Moreover my parents have assured me that I actually fell off my bike against the house and my brother ran up to help me. Strands of this memory are accurate and indeed it still encapsulates part of my childhood, for my brother and I spent much of that time fighting. Yet even this is not clear, for that is the 'myth' I grew up with, namely, that we brothers were always fighting; but the many peaceful and quiet moments are now unrepresented in my memory.

This single memory refers to a complex mixture of present and past feeling, the 'truth' of what actually happened and the overarching story of how I visualize my childhood. Some of this is now told as I answer my own children's question, 'Daddy, how did you get that scar?' In the same way, as we participate in the eucharistic service of remembrance, there is a complex combining of past and present. If we are to be fully open to God's presence amongst us, we must be sensitive to the varied ways God meets with us in the eucharist. An important task for leaders and worshippers is not to shut themselves off from the various means of grace.

God unstops our ears

There are those who approach the eucharist as a time to be reminded of God's truth. The awesome and majestic nature of solemn worship will convey the grandeur of God's law under which we live. The very formality of worship, which is so resented at times, is essential to this approach, for this expresses the objectivity and permanence of God's decrees for us. The parts of the liturgy which concentrate on this are the reciting of the commandments before the confession, the creed and the eucharistic prayer. Whereas these may appear to others as impersonal and cold elements, some will particularly meet with God in these. For as the truth of God is heard, so the call to obedience is proclaimed. Discipleship is possible once God's will is made clearly known.

It is surprising that so many worshippers who were used to a regular diet of matins and evensong easily made the transition to eucharistic worship. But some did, for they could find in both types of liturgy this same proclamation of God's truth. Moreover in the eucharist we are specifically fulfilling the Lord's command to 'do this in remembrance of me'. At a deeper level the truth of God cannot be expressed in timeless commands and ordinances but is found in a description of the life and work of Jesus. The worship that most closely reminds us of God's activity in Christ must actively involve the worshippers. God's truth is indeed our truth as well. This finds expression in the new forms of responsorial creeds. The respected ancient credal statements are interwoven with the sense of making a personal response. This combination is appreciated by many.

> Do you believe and trust in God the Father,
> who made all things?
> **I believe in God, the Father almighty,**
> **creator of heaven and earth.**
>
> Do you believe and trust in his Son Jesus Christ,
> who redeemed the world?
> **I believe in Jesus Christ, his only Son, our Lord.**
> **He was conceived by the power of the Holy Spirit**
> **and born of the Virgin Mary.**
> **He suffered under Pontius Pilate,**
> **was crucified, died and was buried.**
> **He descended to the dead.**
> **On the third day he rose again.**
> **He ascended into heaven,**
> **and is seated at the right hand of the Father.**
> **He will come again to judge the living and the**
> **dead.**

Do you believe and trust in the Holy Spirit,
who gives life to the people of God?
I believe in the Holy Spirit,
the holy catholic Church,
the communion of saints,
the forgiveness of sins,
the resurrection of the body,
and the life everlasting.

This is the faith of the Church.
This is our faith.
We believe in one God,
Father, Son and Holy Spirit.
                                        (*Patterns for Worship*)

God stirs our hearts

A different approach has been experienced by many in a round-about way. In a time of growing ecumenical co-operation many congregations found the formal rules on inter-communion restrictive. So, informal gatherings were promoted, under the title 'agape', a Greek word for love, combining some of the elements of eucharistic worship: a shared meal, a social time and prayers. Participants found in this setting far greater opportunities to express and experience the feelings of mutual respect, warmth and love that properly exist between fellow believers. This in turn renewed their understanding of the eucharist as a time when God moves us deeply within. The communal outward expression of this is at the Peace.

Increasingly parishes are using the Peace in non-eucharistic family services. This raises an important question about the theology of the eucharist. For we are seeking to describe how God meets with us both *in* and *through* the eucharist. That is, the eucharist provides the occasion and the instrument for God to be present with us. Therefore the Peace can be used as a liturgical act on various occasions but it achieves its full significance in the setting of the eucharist. This is so because only in that context is the Peace seemingly brought into relationship with the sacrifice of Christ which establishes our peace. Sacramental worship, which always works on a multitude of levels, is the necessary setting to appreciate the depth of the sign of Peace.

More use can be made of this distinction between occasion and instrument. Most worship will begin with some form of greeting. Some leaders will use this opportunity to begin to arouse feelings in the congregation that they deem appropriate for worship. Whereas I want to affirm the importance of emotion in worship, the practice of some leaders is more akin to the warm-up comic that is brought on before the star performer. In the eucharist we need to remember that God is the one who touches our hearts. It is the leader's task so to present the words of the liturgy that God can use these to stir our hearts.

God opens our eyes

I was introduced to another approach by having to lead a communion service in the local church junior school. Without much time or thought possible before the first occasion, we decided to use a slightly shortened form of Rite A. But this was not appropriate for the children since it encapsulated the approaches described above. One was too distant and remote, the other did not ring true to their situation of being members of the same school, but *not* the same congregation. The part of the service that was appreciated was the presentation of gifts. As well as bringing the bread and wine to the altar, one member of each class brought an example of their school work as an offering. This was received at the altar and blessed as an offering to God. In a beautiful way this brought to light a sense of consecration. By one small piece of work being offered and accepted by God, the whole of life was made holy – not only for the individual child but for the school as well.

Reflecting on that experience I came to see that children pray with their eyes open, sometimes literally, sometimes meta-phorically. A eucharist came alive for them as we celebrated what was clear and immediately visible to them. The eucharistic prayer that matches this experience by using poetic yet direct language is found in *Patterns for Worship*, a subsequent version of which follows:

> The Lord be with you
> **and also with you**.
>
> Lift up your hearts.
> **We lift them to the Lord**.
>
> Let us give thanks to the Lord our God.
> **It is right to give him thanks and praise**.
>
> Blessed are you, Lord God, our light and our salvation;
> > to you be glory and praise for ever!
>
> From the beginning you have created all things
> > and all your works echo the silent music of your praise.
>
> In the fulness of time you made us in your image,
> > the crown of all creation.
>
> You give us breath and speech that with all the powers of heaven
> > we may find a voice to sing your praise:
> > > **Holy, holy, holy Lord,**
> > > **God of power and might,**
> > > **heaven and earth are full of your glory.**
> > > **Hosanna in the highest.**
> > > **Blessed is he who comes in the name of the Lord.**
> > > **Hosanna in the highest.**
>
> How wonderful the work of your hands, O Lord!
> As a mother tenderly gathers her children
> > you embraced a people as your own.
>
> You filled them with longing for a peace without fear,
> > a justice that would never fail.
>
> **To you be praise and glory for ever!**
> From them you raised up Jesus, our Saviour, born of Mary,
> > to be the living bread, in whom all our hungers are satisfied.
>
> He offered his life for sinners,
> > and with a love stronger than death
> > he opened wide his arms on the cross.
>
> **To you be praise and glory for ever!**
> On the night before he suffered on the cross,
> > he came to table with his friends,
> > he took bread, saying,
> > > 'Take this, all of you, and eat.
> > > This is my body which will be given up for you.'

To you be praise and glory for ever!
After supper, he took the cup, and giving thanks, he said:
 'Take this, all of you, and drink my blood of the new
  covenant,
  shed for you and for all, that sins may be forgiven.'
To you be praise and glory for ever!

Christ has died:
Christ is risen:
Christ will come again.

Father, we plead with confidence his sacrifice made
  once for all on the cross,
 we remember his dying and rising in glory,
  and we rejoice that he prays for us at your right hand:
Pour out your Holy Spirit over us and these your gifts
 which we bring before you from your own creation;
Show them to be for us the body and blood of your
  dear Son.
May we who eat and drink in his presence
 be constant in prayer and strong in love
  until all creation is one in Christ.
To you be praise and glory for ever!
Through him, with him, and in him,
with all who stand before you in earth and heaven,
we worship you, Father almighty,
in songs of everlasting praise:
 Blessing and honour and glory and power
 be yours for ever and ever. Amen.

This praying that rejoices in seeing, feeling, touching and giving was opened to me by children, but is not restricted to them. For reasons we will explore later there are theological difficulties with this approach, but for many it is how God reveals himself to them. George Herbert encapsulates this in his poem 'Teach me, my God and King', and in a similar way G. K. Chesterton places grace not just before meals but everywhere:

You say grace before meals.
All right.
But I say grace before the play and the opera,
and grace before the concert and the pantomime,
and grace before I open the book,
and grace before sketching and painting,

in swimming, fencing, boxing, walking, playing, dancing, and grace before I dip pen in the ink.

God restores our vision

If at times we need our eyes open to pray, at other times we need to look beyond what we can see and find our place in eternity. The eucharist can be a reminder of our place within God's overall plan for creation. Primarily in the eucharistic prayer, which should be consonant in style with the whole eucharist, we hear the story of God's work from the beginning to the end. Each particular moment finds its significance as it takes its place in God's overall plan. At each eucharist worshippers are renewed by being brought into relationship with

- the beginning of the story: we see ourselves again as part of God's creation, which God declares to be 'very good';
- the centre: our lives are redeemed because of Jesus' sacrifice and self-offering on the cross;
- the end: we are being saved as God prepares us for his everlasting kingdom.

Images for describing life at the end of time that are consistent with modern beliefs about eternal life are difficult to find. This future element of the story is often only sketchily present. Yet here is a modern thanksgiving which combines these elements with a powerful ambiguous use of the word *today*:

> Blessed are you, God of all glory,
> through your Son Jesus Christ.
> His name is Jesus:
> **Because he saves his people from their sins.**
> He will be called Emmanuel:
> **God is with us. Alleluia!**
> Let us praise the Lord, the God of Israel:
> **He has come to his people and set them free.**
> He gave up all the glory of heaven:
> **and took the nature of a servant.**
> In humility he walked the path of obedience:
> **to die on the cross.**

God raised him to the highest place above
and gave him the name above every name:
Jesus Christ is Lord!
So all beings in heaven and earth will fall at his feet,
and proclaim to the glory of God:
Jesus Christ is Lord!
Today Christ is born:
Alleluia!
Today the Saviour has come:
Alleluia!
Today the angels sing on earth:
Alleluia! Glory to God in the highest!
So, with angels and archangels,
and all the company of heaven,
we praise you for ever, saying
Holy, holy, holy Lord,
God of power and might,
heaven and earth are full of your glory.
Hosanna in the highest.

(Patterns for Worship)

I have described how we can approach the eucharist, and thereby recognize how we meet with God, under four headings. Clearly these titles have been taken from the prophecy in Isaiah, chapter 35, that is such a source of renewal and comfort:

Then the eyes of the blind shall be opened,
and the ears of the deaf unstopped;
then the lame shall leap like a deer,
and the tongue of the speechless sing for joy.
For waters shall break forth in the wilderness,
and streams in the desert.

Jesus is reported as using this prophecy as a description of his own work (Matthew 11.5; Luke 7.22) and so the words have great depth of meaning, referring to the work of God before and in Christ. But other categories could have been used. Drawing on Jesus' description of the first commandment (Mark 12.30) it would be possible to analyse the eucharist as enabling and empowering us to love God with all our heart, mind, soul and strength. Whichever categories are used, the point is the same: God is present to us in all aspects of our lives and all humanity is presented to him through this service.

So the first challenge for composers and leaders of worship is to enrich each approach. With imagination and creativity leaders will want to pay attention to, for example, the physical surroundings of worship, the movement of the people, the placing of icons and candles, the colour of tapestries and vestments – all of which will lead those with eyes open to see God more clearly. Leaders will want to seek out from the congregation a variety of experience of approaching God so that the service may be enriched. My experience has been that candidates preparing for confirmation who have yet to receive communion already know something of how it will move them even if they do not yet have the words to describe it. The second challenge is for each leader to know his or her own blind spot and be able to give space for that in worship.

For the eucharist is not only about remembering but is also the time when our remembering can be healed. These two aspects are combined when we talk of God working through the eucharist to *restore* us and *transform* us. Set in the context of a meal, the image of restoration, nourishment, strengthening is easy to understand. Each time we meet with God we are forgiven, replenished and commissioned to go out in love and service. But this image can develop into a self-understanding of working hard 'in the world' from Monday to Saturday, slowly being drained and compromised, and then returning to God in the Sunday eucharist to be filled again with peace and power. I have heard such words used time and again; whereas they match the immediate experience of worshippers, God is at work in a deeper way as well. For God not only gives us strength to perform his commands but also moulds us into the people who want what he commands. The confession from the Book of Common Prayer contains the words 'we have left undone those things we ought to have done'. As we are transformed into the people that God would have us be, the possibility of doing the things we ought to do becomes more and more ours.

It would be naïve to think that a group meeting to enrich the eucharist in a variety of approaches will be able to avoid conflict. Indeed, many times history has seen one theological truth being pitted against another. For example, any orthodox description of the saving event of the cross will describe it as the work of God done for us and, in no sense, by us. This is mirrored in the eucharist by the emphasis on the all-sufficient sacrifice of Christ and by the sense of God offering himself to us through Christ in the bread and wine. However, it was my experience in the school communion service that showed me so clearly our human need to offer to God. As we bring to God the work of our hands and lives, we appreciate even more what God in turn offers to us. Yet some find this encroaches on the first truth that it is God, not us, who offers himself in the eucharist. It is sad that one truth is being used to exclude another, for both have sound theological backing. So the work of enriching the eucharist in the parish will have to take conflict seriously and be prepared to do careful theological work as well. The words that can be said at the time of offering are anathema to some and a joy to others:

> Blessed are you, Lord God of all Creation,
> through your goodness we have this bread to offer,
> which earth has given and human hands have made.
> It will become for us the Bread of Life.
> **Blessed be God for ever.**
>
> (Roman Missal)

Rejection of these words by some has turned into acceptance when the significance of the final line has been unfolded. It is common in biblical language to find God referred to in a roundabout way, for example, in this case, by using the passive voice. 'It will become . . . ' effectively means 'God will make it for us . . . '. Thus the prayer of blessing affirms throughout the activity of God, even if it refers at another level to our offering.

To end this part on a brighter note, let us look at one example where words from a recent piece of liturgical writing complement the rather negative feelings expressed in an older passage. The Prayer of Humble Access contains the sentence 'We are not worthy so much as to gather up the crumbs under your table'. This is evocative, drawing on words of Jesus and expressing theological truth, but leaves many who say the prayer uncomfortable and resentful. For those whose self-esteem is low may not be moved by these words into closer communion with God. Yet the third eucharistic prayer picks up the same words and confidently prays 'We thank you for counting us worthy'. This manages to combine the proclamation of human worth with the truth that this worth originates in God. On Sundays when we use the Prayer of Humble Access, we always use the third eucharistic prayer!

Part 2

Expectations

People have a right to expect something to happen at the eucharist, but the eucharist is not a tame domestic pet that reacts to all our whims. More important, there are some fundamental truths about the eucharist which defy neat categorization. The language of the liturgy is that of 'assiduous supposing'; in other words, the prayers ask things that are beyond words, and speak about truths which cannot be encapsulated into human converse. But that does not mean that we should give up trying. Again, whereas baptism takes place once in a person's life, the eucharist is repeated. We enter the covenant at the font, but renew it at the table. That balance needs adjusting nowadays, when there is talk of 'repeating' baptism, which is contrary to Scripture, against tradition, and makes nonsense of any rational approach to the essential difference between these two central sacraments. The eucharist, therefore, has a life of its own. It is not possible to confine it to our environment. But it lives alongside us, and rejoices in our world. In that sense, it is a sacrament of the incarnation. On the other hand, it relies on the once-and-for-all act of love on the cross, which is unrepeatable – like baptism. Yet it bears repetition, because we have been commanded to repeat it (1 Corinthians 11.23–26).

Repetition is linked to frequency, and the question of how much is appropriate and good for us. In bygone days, there was a certain reserve about receiving communion. Roman Catholics for many centuries until our own received rarely. Even the great and devout of the seventeenth century were only accustomed to a monthly eucharist. In my childhood I well remember matins as the main service most Sunday mornings. It made the eucharist special. Now things are different, but they are not the worse for it.

We have drawn attention in these pages to the importance of mystery and imagination. These are key terms in the eucharistic vocabulary. For they explain two areas of understandable frustration that many worshippers experience, whether within minutes of being confirmed or later on when they receive a fairly heavy spiritual jolt. The first is the gap between worship as it is experienced and life as it is lived in ordinary terms. The second is the gap between the vision of the world that Christianity proclaims and the dull and dark reality that it so often becomes.

I suspect that these two gaps play a large part in people's hopes and feelings when they move around homes, shopping-centres, offices, staff-rooms and sanctuaries, week by week. It is not possible to be a sane, contemporary, aware human being without feeling some degree of anguish at the way worship is sometimes celebrated – and then to compare *that* with the life that is actually lived in those homes, shopping-centres, offices and staff-rooms. Similarly, it is not possible to be a sane, contemporary, aware human being without feeling an equal degree of disenchantment at being told what the promises of God are and what one has to put up with as a very second best. And the fact of the matter is that many people throw in the sponge and give up, either by stopping going to church altogether or by going along occasionally as a way of 'hanging in there'.

If the eucharist is really a way of expressing what the Church is in terms of feeding on the Lord and proclaiming his death until the end of all time, then it has to grapple with these gaps. And the way it does so is by repetition in context. The eucharist has been celebrated in all kinds of different contexts from the earliest times until now. Go into an ancient church and it is hard not to be moved by the thoughts that this is sacred ground on which the eucharist was offered by young men going off to the crusades, wealthy burghers at the Renaissance, and distraught naval ratings' spouses during the Falklands conflict. Similarly, go into an anonymous, bare and functional common room in a college and someone may tell you that there was an informal communion here this morning before most people arrived, and everything was quickly packed away and removed so that the eucharistic germ of that community might not obtrude into the life of the whole, but remain content to be a prophetic sign of that inner motivation which we sometimes call the Holy Spirit.

Repetition is sometimes covered by differences of style – such as those we have just described. It is also expressed by the varieties of preaching that are offered: who would give the same sermon to a house group as to a Sunday assembly? But there is one particular way in which repetition weighs heavily – and flexibly – on the eucharistic community, wherever and whatever its kind, and that is in the business of the prayers of intercession.

Intercessions

The intercessions have had a long and interesting history. They died a bit of a death in the Middle Ages, only to experience something of a resuscitation when the 'bidding of the bedes' (the vernacular devotions after the sermon) became popular in the centuries just before the Reformation. In nearly all the revised liturgies of the Western world, they have appeared as a flexible form in which the Church is able to give voice to its earnest prayers on behalf of the Christian community, the leaders of the nations, the suffering and the departed. Unlike past centuries, where the prayer-forms were relatively fixed, the intercessions used today usually come in free structures. This is a sign of the times: the intercession must not be strait-jacketed. It could be said without much contradiction that the two *freest* places in the liturgy are the sermon and the intercessions.

Why intercede? Why not just give up and let live? *This* is the issue of all issues that underlies the frustrations caused by those two gaps mentioned earlier. For the intercession, so far from being an exercise in trying to get God to change his mind, is our statement that God *cares*. He may not give all the answers. He does not distribute gifts fairly (which is not the same as *freely*). He may not even appear to answer all our prayers – for the sense of the absence of God is for many people a necessary and at times horribly real part of their life of faith. Right through the gospels we have pictures of Jesus being with people in their pain and anguish, as well as sharing in their joys and their achievements. To intercede before God is to join our prayers with those of Christ himself in heaven (Hebrews 4.14–16). That image of Christ as the high priest in heaven is not in the New Testament for the sake of coining a fancy scene. It is there because it expresses the way in which God draws the whole world in its present imperfections and weaknesses into the power of his love.

That makes intercession a way of standing back from the world, with one foot in heaven. So all intercessions are going to be as 'assiduous' in their 'supposing' as we may ever wish. And at the eucharist, intercessions are going to have to have a certain healthy detachment about them, not in the sense of not caring, but because the eucharist is itself a statement of how the world is made new, continuing to live in a world not yet fully transformed. I therefore listen intently to intercessions. Sometimes they seem like news bulletins – but, then, the congregation needs to know certain facts. Sometimes they seem to make assumptions which I would be loath to make – but, then, we are all different. And there are also times when they breathe a warm devotion before the presence of God sadly lacking in some of our structured, official prayer-forms. You cannot win! If there is one theme regularly absent, it is the mention of the saints and heaven – another mirror of our utilitarian culture. There is a beautiful collect that sometimes concludes the intercessions in the American Book of Common Prayer (1979) which makes this point eloquently:

Hasten, O Father, the coming of your kingdom; and grant that we your servants, who now live by faith, may with joy behold your Son at his coming in glorious majesty; even Jesus Christ, our only Mediator and Advocate.

The eucharist: window on past, present and future

It is not possible to limit the eucharist, but every age has a good try. One perhaps helpful perspective is to see the Lord's Supper as embodying three ways of looking at time and eternity. We here speak of the eucharist as memorial of Christ's death, as renewal of the covenant, and as united with Christ's prayer in heaven. These three angles on time neatly draw together past, present and future. Not that they are self-contained, but they focus on a particular time-scale. Negatively, it is important to make the point that to say that the eucharist *only* remembers Christ's death runs the risk of nailing it to the cross; to say that the eucharist *only* renews the covenant now runs the risk of detaching it from its roots; and to say that the eucharist *only* unites with Christ in heaven is to give it an unduly futurist perspective. To put it at its sharpest, we badly need all three, because to celebrate the holy communion is to look back to Calvary, to be the Christian community in the here and now, and also to be in love with the future.

To speak of 'the memorial of his saving passion', as one of the eucharistic prayers puts it, is to say more than that the Lord's Supper 'remembers' a past event. The table of the Lord is not a regimental dinner. The notion of 'memorial' of the eucharist has stronger nuances than simply a psychological or mental process. Indeed, one of the things preachers have alerted congregations to across the years is the danger of internalizing the eucharist. To remember is to perform an action, because an action has an objectivity to it. The memory is deep and profound and to remember Christ is to return to someone we knew already. The eucharist touches the collective unconscious of the Christian community. That is why we can latch on to the saints, both living and departed, because they are and have been one of the means whereby God reaches us in Christ. The memory exists in time and is, as Augustine wrote in *Confessions*, 'the stomach of the mind'. It is also a 'rich cavern' which is fitted out with all kinds of treasures.

To celebrate the memory of Christ is an action of the eternal God in human time. The centrality of the cross is fundamental, for that is the motivating factor behind the eucharist, a proclamation of the dying and rising Lord. So strong can this notion of memory become that there are some Eastern liturgies which 'remember' not only the past events, such as Christ's death and burial, and his present actions, such as his intercession at the Father's right hand, but also sweep on to the future and actually 'remember' his second coming. This is no error of language or conceptual mistake. It is simply the result of locating that 'remembering' in the total memory of the Church, as it were, standing outside itself.

Secondly, the eucharist is also a renewal of the covenant by the people of God, for Christ's blood is shed as the blood of that new and everlasting covenant (1 Corinthians 11.25). A covenant is a binding agreement between friends, and it is at the altar of God that the Christian community is able to renew its solidarity with each other and with God. To speak in such a way as this may at first sight seem bland, but it strikes at the heart of what we said earlier about repetition. God *always* offers another chance. The reason why Christians need a way of entering, and of renewing, that covenant is that it is a covenant in which we are in constant need of God's forgiving grace. This grace is not about being perfect so much as about coming to terms with our imperfections. It is not about striving actively to be better and better every day so much as about walking in a 'newness of life' (to quote the old Prayer Book) wherein we can keep falling and getting up again. The agreement that God makes with us in Jesus Christ is not about denying our humanity. It is rather about affirming it, of seeing beauty in its scars, wonder in its limitations, and the seeds of eternity in the blemishes that we know all too well.

A repeated renewal of that covenant can only lead to one

response, which Paul expresses in a wonderful passage towards the end of his letter to the Romans:

> I appeal to you therefore, brethren, by the mercies of God, to present your bodies as a living sacrifice, holy and acceptable to God, which is your spiritual worship. Do not be conformed to this world but be transformed by the renewal of your mind, that you may prove what is the will of God, what is good and acceptable and perfect. (Romans 12.1, 2)

A sacrifice that is living is, at first sight, a contradiction in terms. But in the context of the cross, the Christian's 'living sacrifice' is nothing more and nothing less than a self-sacrifice, to offer 'our souls and bodies', as the prayer after communion often puts it. The offering is a real one, in the sense that it *costs*, not as much as Calvary, for that would be to place ourselves on a par with Christ! But the cost is the taking up of our cross to follow Christ, taking up his lead, and taking our place in the communion of saints as we journey through history into the heavenly Jerusalem. To offer ourselves is to say that we have seen the vision of something that has touched us so deeply, we have had its memory activated inside us so profoundly, that we want to align ourselves with the things of God yet again, knowing full well that we will need to come back for more. To renew that binding agreement and to feast together with delight is to say that the eucharist has a present focus that draws us back to the world and to the context of which we are a part already. There will be times when this latter aspect is all too apparent.

That is the challenge of the sacrifice that is living – not to ignore what we know to be familiar, but to be transformed in our way of relating to it. I can think of many severe problems in my own life that have been constantly and painfully fed and gradually relieved by dogged persistence at prayer and eucharist. It was not always easy, and there were moments when I felt myself drawn into a cynical shell of complacency, but I found God there somehow, speaking in the deep silence, and I found him not just beside me but ahead of me, helping me to renew that covenant in the blood of his Son.

Memory and covenant point us to past and present. What calls us to the future? There are many images of the future in the Bible, like the mustard seed (Matthew 13.31). But the real pointer to the future must also be Christ, who is the same yesterday, today and for ever (Hebrews 13.8). For this reason, his prayer in heaven for us (Hebrews 7.23–25) is a powerful image of the way in which our world is held in the arms of God. We drew attention earlier to this picture as the foundation of all intercession. But it is more than that. For the presence of Christ at the Father's right hand is nothing more than a way of painting in a colourful style the sheer fact of Christ *being with us* before God. His 'prayers' cannot be like ours – but ours are heard through him. And that gives all our prayers more than the sense of being listened to by someone else. Our prayers are part of his being with God, not least when we are doing something which we have been commanded to do. Whether or not Jesus actually did tell his followers to 'do this in memory of me', it is clear that the first Christians found it impossible to live without celebrating the eucharist in some form and with some degree of frequency.

To join our prayers with his eternal offering in heaven is to say that the celebration of holy communion takes the Church onwards along the road to that eternal dwelling-place. The road to the future may be rugged and hard; it may be unbearably unpredictable and fraught with danger; it may include missed opportunities (at which the Church sometimes seems to be expert in a cultivated art!). But it is still the pilgrim community on earth keeping its perspectives open for the future, pleading for grace to see those opportunities. That is why in some eucharistic prayers, the word 'plead' appears when the prayer moves from remembering Christ's life and death, resurrection and presence with us now, and looks also to the future. To plead Christ's sacrifice is to ensure that we look at everything, past, present and future, through the cross, which is the heart of the new creation.

These three dimensions form a key foundation for the way we look at the Lord's Supper. When taken individually, they give a lopsided picture, but when put together they serve us with rich fare. They take the banalities of life as we know it – the Church included! – seriously, but they also lift us up out of that quagmire sometimes referred to as the 'incarnate Church' and the 'naughty world', into a way of living that gives the very humanity of pilgrim community and sinful creation a glistening of gold and the hope of another chance.

What the eucharist can't – and can – do

How do we draw these threads together? The way that teachers used to try to adopt at the school I attended as a little boy was to make a list of 'dos' and 'don'ts'. At the risk of sounding simplistic, I would like to do exactly this. What follows is a mixture of pastoral musings over the years and some gems taken from Jeremy Taylor's *Worthy Communicant*, which was published in 1660 as part of the drive of the Restoration Church to bring the eucharist back into the consciousness of the people.

First of all, what not to do. There are six.

Do not over-scrutinize yourself. There was a time when people underwent elaborate self-examination before communion. I would guess that those days are gone. But I do not think that over-scrutiny has disappeared with it. My hunch is that many people are filled with self-doubt, low self-esteem and a feeling that they have got it all wrong again. People might not examine themselves too much before communion, as was the custom in previous generations, but they will still do it afterwards, forming a kind of mush of self-abnegation. Look first at Christ, as the Saviour who longs to welcome us home (Luke 15.11ff.).

Do not make the sermon more important than the rest of the service. In an age of much talking and public discourse, it is easy to think first and foremost of the sermon at a service. Indeed, there are many churches that publicize who the preacher is going to be, not the president. Perhaps that is right, for the wrong reason! We do not want to make a cult of the president, but the preacher's words are always going to be different – at least we hope that they will be. See the sermon, then, as part of the service, deliberately built up to in the readings, and reflected upon in the prayers. The sermon should not stand out like a sore thumb, seeking its own independent life. Many congregations perhaps need to heed those words in terms of their own response.

Do not pin your hopes to any particular end. Many people who are overtaken by a particular worry – or request – will let these conditions hijack their eucharistic life. I want this, or I don't want that. And a natural desire overtakes life. But the eucharist is corporate and it is a way of sharing other people's sufferings, sometimes brought home in a heart-rending way at the sharing of the Peace with someone recently tragically bereaved. (This example, however, is not meant as an encouragement to smother people spiritually!) Intercessions and intentions at the eucharist are about the discernment of the will of God and about faith in the never-ending ability of God to draw the pieces together, or at least to let them stay apart for a time but to be less unbearable. We may well pray with Augustine, 'Grant what you command and command what you will'. That protest before God is a way of entering his life with us.

Do not ask the eucharist to make you rich. This cannot be said too often in an age in which economic forces seem to be determining everything. I have lived in a wealthy part of the country for some years and, on reflection, I think it is probably salutary that my own economic standards were very different from many of the people around me. My children got used to it years ago, and I am glad to say that they were not bitter about it, because they knew that Rectory life is infinitely more enriching, varied and satisfying than most others. (Allow my bias to show through! People – even regular church-attenders – have curious ideas of what goes on in clerical households.) The eucharist cannot make you rich. All it does is help you to see what is really important.

Do not expect all doubt to disappear. You will remain the

same as you were – but only different. The 'transformation' of which Paul speaks (in Romans 12.2) will never produce the perfect person by this world's standards. I have held out my hands at communion in a state of near-ecstasy when everything in my life cohered and everything around me stood still. But that has only happened a very few times, on occasions I can count on only one hand. There have been more occasions when I have felt dry, routine, empty, depressed, or just slightly restless with myself and my world. My doubts have not disappeared. I have offered them to God. They are part of the humanity he has affirmed in Christ – so he can do with them what he likes.

Do not judge yourself by the moods of passing times. Here we have human nature at its most varied. Some people are more volatile than others. Some are steady as rocks and live in need of more colourful people to enliven their experience. Others are manic-depressives, who need soothing influences around them. And there will be countless others. In an age that likes to analyse according to personality type, there will be surprises. Categorizations will always – like diagnosis of illness – have something of the approximation to them. God lives in the heights and the depths: let him into both.

And now, the things to expect the eucharist to do. Once more, there are six.

Expect the eucharist, as a feast of love, to enable you to live in charity with others. By this I do not mean the ability to be more charitable than other people: no one has prior rights on this quality of life. But the eucharist will provide the security to ensure that charity will figure as an ideal, a means towards greater union with God and other people. People always give of their best – and live at their best – when they are surrounded by love. Sometimes this will involve saying difficult things – the eucharistic prayer 'narrates' a terrifying story of the cross. But love is the root of all that is good and the eucharist has to be a 'love feast'.

Second, the eucharist is one of the ways in which the forgiveness of sins is proclaimed and made known. Although

there are occasions when the confession and absolution are not
appropriate, by and large they are, because to walk 'in newness
of life' (as the Prayer Book describes eucharistic existence) pre-
supposes a turning away from an old, hidden and murky stroll
through time. Forgiveness, however, doesn't always come easy,
and there will be occasions when we have been so hurt that all
we can really do is pray for the *intention* to forgive someone else.
There is no magic – no instant forgiveness. Another reason for
repetition of that Supper. Primarily, however, it starts with
God's forgiveness of *us*.

Third, the eucharist is the greatest act of worship that
Christians can do together. Therefore it has a unique focus
which no other service, however wonderful and worthy and
beautiful, can possibly convey. It is a channel of God's love, a
'conduit-pipe' of his grace. This may well explain the sheer
variety of contexts in which the eucharist has been celebrated
across the centuries. It is so rich that it simply keeps coming
back for more, because its mysterious character actually
prevents it from being in any way 'summarized' by description.
It requires no justification whatever, but for its closeness to
God's nature – and to ours.

Fourth, the Lord's Supper gives us the promise of resurrection to new life. The fact of the celebration, with its symbols of
bread and wine conveying God's presence among us, expresses
the dying and rising of life. In order to create these elements of
food, corn and grapes have to be crushed and turned into
something new which takes on an eternal meaning. This is
God's way of showing that he takes our life and transforms
it. And, as always with the promises of God, the whole future
is not yet fulfilled in the present. The words 'The Body of
Christ keep you in eternal life' have a force that point to a life
in God now.

Fifth, to gather round that table is to keep a healthy
diet. There has been much discussion of frequency over the
centuries. Some traditions are marked by reticence, such as
those members of the Free Kirk in the Scottish Highlands,
where communion is celebrated perhaps twice a year and is

therefore built up to after a great deal of searching and preparation. Similarly, there are those who proclaim eucharistic health by daily communion, so that it becomes their 'daily bread'. Temperaments are going to vary across the religious cultures. But 'repetition' isn't a guarantee for the quality of the product, only a deep-felt expression of commitment and trust. For most people, I would hold that a weekly celebration is the norm; enough for each week, and sufficient for the morrow.

Finally, the eucharist binds the community together in the Lord. Union with Christ is, at the end of the day, the prime reason for sharing that bread and that cup. Between the lines of the New Testament we can read of a strong sense of solidarity in Christ experienced by those who ate and drank in his presence. At its sharpest, followers of Jesus could do no other than break that bread and share that cup. To participate in Christ in the eucharist is the noblest way of saying I am a Christian, because it gives to those who 'draw near with faith' a new way of looking at themselves, the world and Christ himself.

Postscript: a story that never ends

The Church will never manage to tame the eucharist, however hard it may try in one culture or another. In our own day, there are countless opportunities for better liturgies, by which I do not mean places where everything is so neat and well organized that the honest bystander longs for something to go wrong. The opportunities are endless because human beings have a God-given instinct to worship and adore, as well as to struggle with all the problems that are not entirely soluble. 'Hm . . . well, that's a bit difficult', as the visiting speaker at the AGM so eloquently put it.

We are given what we are given. 'Such as will live the life of God must eat the flesh and drink the blood of the Son of Man, because this is a part of that diet which if we want (= lack) we cannot live', wrote Richard Hooker four hundred years ago. But, note, he says 'this is *a* part of that diet' – not the whole diet. If it were the entire diet, we would spend our whole lives in church celebrating the eucharist, a prospect which I for one would find unbearable.

When the dismissal has been given – not an announcement, a command, by the way – I have the prospect of a world that still sags under the weights and measures of human stupidity, warped vision and compromise. But somehow it doesn't matter quite so much, because I have within me the promise of a never-ending life, which I have received not just for myself but for my fellow-humans and the rest of God's creation. So I proceed on my path through human history into eternity. I may not have liked the sermon. I may have felt that the intercessions were a might too worthy. That hymn could have been taken at a different pace. And I do wish that we had a bit more time to think about it all. But it is enough for now – until next time. I mustn't expect to take God in all at once.

Strengthen for service, Lord,
the hands that have taken holy things;
may the ears which have heard your word
be deaf to clamour and dispute;
may the tongues which have sung your praise
be free from deceit;
may the eyes which have seen the tokens of your love
shine with the light of hope;
and may the bodies which have been fed with your body
be refreshed with the fulness of your life; glory to you for ever.

(Malabar Liturgy)

8

c/oc/oc/o

Developing tradition

Imaginative exercise 1
Design a church building that expresses in architecture what
you believe and feel is important about the nature of the
church.

This is an exercise of the imagination. It is not necessary for
every detail to be architecturally sound. Yet the decision about
including some fairly basic ingredients such as doors, heating
and kitchen furniture may reveal significant beliefs about the
nature and purpose of the church as you envisage it. Nor is it
intended that this exercise leads to iconoclasm, tearing down
what is already built, what may be functional but less than
ideal. Yet the exercise of being offered a clean sheet of paper
signifying the chance to make a totally fresh beginning can
release ideas that may change parish buildings. In our parish it
was when we heard a child call the room set aside for the crèche
'the black hole' that we realized change was needed, even if the
room would not be relocated.

One group worked on this exercise and produced a startling
result. We would probably recognize their design for a church
building as an ancient Greek temple. There was a large roofed
area with the roof being supported by a double row of columns
around the perimeter. Inside this double row there was
an open, uncluttered space with a table/altar at one end. No
further facilities or distinguishing marks were present in their
picture. It may not be to everyone's liking but it made some
important comments on how they saw church life.

The most noticeable item was the roof. They wanted the church building to encompass a defined and definite area. The roof provides shelter for all those who enter into the church. This area is defined not by walls nor by doors but by what is found over us, protecting us. As there were no walls, people could come in and out of the church in many directions, thus providing free access in many ways. The double row of the columns provided many open but confined loitering spaces. I could imagine meeting friends in this church 'by the third column on the left'. In this way, there would be the security of being in a familiar place (just as some people sit on the same pew or chair Sunday by Sunday) without 'owning' that particular place, for the space is open to others. Moreover, there would be spaces for people to stay within the protection of the columns and yet be able to see what was happening in the centre.

Earlier in this book we referred to the practice of being present at the eucharist intentionally without receiving communion. Much of this design affirms the importance of accessibility without defining for people the door by which they must enter, nor how far they must go. If they are to enter this church and then proceed further into the inner space, the life and worship that is offered there has to be good enough to draw people further in. That is one challenge that I hear, as a leader of worship, in this design.

Syracuse Cathedral in Sicily is based on an old Greek temple. Over the last 1,600 years much of the interior decoration and artifacts have been changed and, especially, accumulated. But it is still possible to see that the essential framework of the church building is an old temple. Significantly, the gaps between the outer row of columns have all been filled in except for one, thus making this the one entrance into the church. Between these two columns has been placed a large wooden door. As I visited this church it was very easy to see and feel the restrictions that have been placed on access to the holy place and its worship. If this building were in England, there would probably be a sign on the door saying why it was locked and where the key could be found!

As we have raised throughout this book the issue of access there has been the accompanying matter of those who have power or influence over granting access to the church. It is very easy to criticize those in power for exercising it in a restrictive way. But we have clearly located this power to enable access in the Church as a whole and not merely in the ordained ministers. Paul describes Apollos, Cephas and himself as 'stewards of the mysteries of God' (1 Corinthians 4.1), and by implication he applies this to all ministers. Yet there is much in today's descriptions of the Body of Christ that indicates that all baptized Christians share in this ministry. Some may have particular gifts and roles in ordering worship, but all can contribute to the work of making available the mysteries of God. Discussion about this exercise within a group revealed to me the importance of the symbol of the door into church – and that the role of doorkeeper is given to us all.

Before we leave this example of an answer to the imaginative exercise, I want to rehabilitate the symbol of doors or walls. For earlier we have noted that it can be superficial to see access as a right of everyone; or to put it another way, that the stewards do not have the right to deny access. However, if we have begun to appreciate the mystery and majesty of God that is made present in the eucharist and other forms of worship, we have a responsibility as stewards of this mystery to make apparent what is on the other side of the door. Worship is more than an order of words, a means of instruction, or a pattern of self-fulfilment. As the uninitiated enter into church life they deserve the message carefully given: kneel here, be still and pray, for here prayer is already valid. The door is narrow, not to restrict access, but to slow down the spiritual tourists so that they too can experience the church as a place to meet with God.

In his rule for ordering monastic life, Benedict said:

> Do not grant newcomers to the monastic life an easy entry . . . If someone comes and keeps knocking at the door, and if at the end of four or five days, he has shown himself patient in bearing . . . difficulty of entry, and has persisted in his request, then he should be allowed to enter. (Chapter 58)

We are all challenged to combine the message of welcome and mystery in what we build and say and do.

> *Imaginative exercise 2*
> *Write a prayer, for personal devotion or corporate use, for the moment in the eucharist after receiving communion and before the final blessing and dismissal.*

Many people have identified that there is a rather abrupt ending to the Rite A eucharist. The Book of Common Prayer uses the Lord's Prayer and the Gloria directly after receiving communion so devotion is lifted into praise before being closed by the blessing. But there is only one set prayer in Rite A which bears the whole weight of closure. In a few succinct lines, the prayer combines thanks to God for feeding, the offer of a living sacrifice and a request to be sent out. Whereas the prayer itself is concise, the flow of liturgy is minimal. Some complain that they hardly have time to settle into the prayer before they are being commissioned to 'go in peace'. No wonder then that in many congregations the prayer 'Father of all' is said all together rather than being reserved for the president alone. If communicants are to make a helpful, gentle transition from the table to the world outside, then more needs to be available at this point in the liturgy. The rubric authorizes various prayers to be used.

This exercise invites you to compose a prayer for such use. You may wish to take the form of a personal prayer of devotion. This would express to God, for example, personal gratitude for a mutual drawing together in worship, the hope that the full benefit of communion would be revealed in daily living and/or the desire to continue in an awareness of God's presence throughout the coming week. However, as the service is drawing to its close, the pattern of the liturgy would be better suited by a corporate prayer; that is, we need to express what we have done together, even if this has affected us deeply as separate individuals. It is interesting to note that the set prayer 'Almighty God, we thank you for feeding us . . . ' is essentially a private prayer said all together, for 'we/us/our' can be replaced by 'I/me/my' and the prayer still makes sense. Yet 'Father of all' is necessarily a prayer of the congregation or church, for it speaks on behalf of 'we and all your children'. By deciding which form to use, you will be expressing something of how you visualize God at work, whether it is primarily through the Body which is composed of individuals or through individual Christians who can and often do work collectively.

As you do this exercise, you will be drawing on the Christian tradition for words, thoughts and feelings. Some people value extempore prayer as the most authentic form of prayer because it allows the spirit to speak through what is spontaneous, fresh and new. Speaking personally, as I listen to my own spontaneous prayers week by week I notice how clearly they follow a pattern and how seldom I am surprised by my own words. Certain topics will always feature in my extempore intercessions and by implication I know that I must be blind to other aspects of God's world. So there is virtue in 'prepared spontaneity' – the delivery should have an immediate feeling. But because this is not the first time you have come to the end of a eucharist, you already know the sort of experience you will be wanting to express. The Christian tradition is there to help you do just this. You can draw on words from the Bible, famous hymns, poetry or other devotional writing. Plagiarism in composing prayers is not a crime, for the more you use words that already have a history of being prayed the richer and more resonant will be your own prayer.

This draws attention to one of the undercurrents of this book: our life of worship will be enriched as we are more able and ready to draw on our Christian inheritance. I have always found the most disappointing part of the ASB to be the small section 'Prayers for various occasions' (pp. 99–107). This contains no more than a few collects and some revised prayers from the Book of Common Prayer. It is not (and perhaps could not be within the ASB in that format) a small treasury of devotions that could be referred to by any worshipper to supplement the formal liturgy and in times of quiet. So when certain parishes have printed their own worship booklet containing, for example, Rite A, they have included within the text, or alongside as a running commentary, other prayers (old and new). These may never be spoken aloud but they are available to be used by all as required. This symbolizes in print the important relationship of formal liturgy texts to the devotion of the past and present. We need to become more familiar with books of prayers not because the knowledge of God is found in words from the past, but so that we may have a better vocabulary to express our experience of God in the present.

Referring back to the first imaginative exercise, you may see that many aspects have been drawn from traditional architecture. Indeed, the example we discussed draws on pre-Christian building. We can have more confidence in our faith, our liturgy and our architecture now if we consciously know how others have reacted to the presence of God in their midst before. Confidence seems sadly lacking in many denominations now because there is a feeling that we are facing such a range of troubles that have not been faced before. But we can pick up on the clue when today's generation is called 'the beginning of the new dark age'. The Church came through the destruction of the Roman Empire and the beginning of the Dark Ages and soon found itself in a period of liturgical and ecclesiastical innovation. So an important part of preparing a new prayer is learning what has been said before, then using a new vocabulary to say what is right for our own context. In Chapter 3 we have drawn attention to how this is already happening within formal liturgy by lay people preparing intercessions. This exercise is another example of pointing to what is missing and so preparing the way for the liturgy of tomorrow.

Finally, the moment in the eucharist for which you are asked to compose a prayer has intentionally been chosen as a 'boundary' moment. Worshippers are leaving communion and the table and preparing to move across into 'ordinary life'. The moment could be called 'from table to kingdom' except this could convey that the table (and eucharistic worship) is not also part of the kingdom. Describing this moment and our associated spiritual needs is not at all easy. The phrase 'send us out into the world' was simplified to 'send us out' in the post-communion prayer (although the longer phrase is still preserved in the authorized alternative para. 86 of Rite A), thus removing the connotations that the world is outside and we belong 'inside'. Even the well-received alternative 'Father of all' contains phrases that convey to some extent an over-emphasis on the life and light that is found within the Body of Christ: 'bring life to others', 'give light to the world'. There is no acknowledgement of God's love and light that can be found outside the fellowship of believers.

In his book on ordained ministry, Robin Greenwood stresses the need to find a picture of the Church 'that understands how to be both challenging and consoling to society, also knows how to receive challenge and consolation from society'. The emphasis that can so often be forgotten in liturgy is the need for Christians to leave worship in order to seek and find what God is already doing in his kingdom. We need to understand and pray about this boundary. You can offer new words for this.

Imaginative exercise 3
Suppose that your church has organized a ten-week course on the basic Christian faith for enquirers. You receive a telephone call 15 minutes before a session is about to begin, telling you that the leader has just been taken ill and cannot attend the meeting. You are asked to drop everything and immediately lead the session titled 'Living in the Kingdom – a Christian understanding of heaven'. On the spur of the moment, what would you want to talk about?

We have drawn attention on a number of occasions to the way that the eucharist is more than the sum of the parts. So also the Church of God involves more than every living Christian, every building or Christian organization. There is more to worship than what we see or say, what we understand or control. Thus the movement that leads to a simplification of worship and its language for the purpose of proclaiming the message more clearly has left spiritual gaps that need to be filled. Some words and images need to be left 'lying around' in the liturgy, for we cannot determine precisely what meaning they may deliver or what devotion they may evoke. Stanislavsky, the great director, recommended that a revolver be left on the stage, for no one could know who might want to use it one day.

We need to regain access to the beliefs and devotion surrounding 'the communion of saints', the future kingdom of God and heaven. This will not be done by providing clear teaching or precise formulations, for this area more than most needs a poetic language that is more at home with visions than facts. Yet the need is great. On the two occasions I have preached tentatively about what may happen to us after death and the nature of God's judgement, I have received an over-whelming response showing interest, worry and concern. Some Christians have admitted to me, with a sense of unashamed guilt, that they have been drawn to contact mediums and spiritualists because the Church has nothing to say on this matter. They know their need for help to make sense of their unreflected beliefs and would rather the Church met this need, but they will seek out help elsewhere if the Church is unwilling to engage in discussion.

So in this exercise you are asked to outline your understanding of heaven. The point of imagining the situation of your being suddenly asked to do this is to direct your thoughts to what you already believe rather than what you think the Church teaches on this subject. At a later stage you may want to study further the different approaches that have been made through the history of the Church and so be able to draw on tradition. For now, you are asked to think about your intuitive beliefs. These are likely to have taken shape either in your own times of bereavement and closeness to death or during worship as you have come across formal liturgical language or hymnody. Look at these words taken from a hymn by Isaac Watts which has been given the subtitle 'A prospect of heaven makes death easy'.

> There is a land of pure delight,
> where saints immortal reign;
> infinite day excludes the night,
> and pleasures banish pain.

There everlasting spring abides,
and never-withering flowers;
death, like a narrow sea, divides
that heavenly land from ours.

These words may have good associations for some, but it is clear that they could provoke such an adverse reaction in you that your own beliefs begin to crystallize. This is what you are being asked to put into words so that others can be helped, and that together we can find an authentic and honest vocabulary for heaven.

For the Church is very vulnerable on this subject. I have already mentioned how not having anything to say leaves people with an important unmet need. Yet if talk about heaven becomes too ideal, the Church is criticized for promising 'pie in the sky' and being 'no earthly good'; if the talk becomes too realistic, we can be criticized for straying from heaven to hell and being judgemental. However, much of the material for the Advent season in *The Promise of His Glory* seems to strike the right balance by being visionary and imaginative while also clearly inviting a response from worshippers here and now. We may be vulnerable on this subject, and not all our attempts to encapsulate the truth will be successful, but this is a task worth doing.

Let me offer an example: imagine your manager puts his head around the door and says 'The tax inspectors are coming in tomorrow'. Your reaction could rightly be sheer panic: 'I'm going to be found out.' Indeed, who does not pass a traffic warden on the pavement without looking at the clock even though you know that you left your car only five minutes ago? This fear in the face of judgement rightly leads us to a sense of confession and penitence for what is wrong. If God our judge is coming again, now is the time to confess. I know a tax inspector who uses the opening line 'Is there anything else you would like to tell me?' to which the only reply seems to be 'Everything'. If we take seriously the harm we can cause by our wrong-doing, then all must be confessed. Yet we project onto tax inspectors and traffic wardens the idea that they are trying to catch us out. Their task is also to uphold the law and what is right. It is clearly part of the biblical understanding of the judge that the judge will side with those who have done no wrong. If we are in the right, the judge will actively declare us to be righteous. So what begins with the reality of fear in the face of judgement ends with God's gift of righteousness in Christ.

Henri Nouwen offers a new approach to understanding the communion of saints in *Our Greatest Gift*. He explores the idea that our death can be also the gift of new life to those left behind. He reflects on the words of John, chapter 16, where Jesus is reported to say 'It is for your own good that I am going, because unless I go, the Spirit will not come to you; but if I do go, I will send him to you'. These words, Nouwen suggests, can be used by us in our dying as well; the meaning is still valid at an 'ordinary' human death and not merely at the one unique death of the Christ. Nouwen describes his experience of those who, at their death, not only bequeath to others their possessions and achievements but also hand over what has been the source of their inspiration and joy in life. Thus 'sending the spirit' can be a good phrase to express the continuity of love which is known and established in life but survives beyond death. Moreover, it is possible for each of us to send the spirit of Christ (not our own spirit) at our death if we have based our lives on Christ. This is part of what we value in the doctrine of the community of saints: that God has made himself known in ordinary human lives and that their example can continue to be an inspiration, a challenge and an encouragement to dedicate our lives to God in Christ. Nouwen acknowledges that using these words of Jesus in this way may sound strange and unfamiliar. But perhaps this use is making freshly available truths that have been expressed in other ways in the past and are now lost to us.

For those who are more at ease with straightforward biblical language, I would like to offer one more example. Revelation, chapter 21, presents a great vision of 'a new heaven and a new earth'. In verses 7 and 8 there is a clear description of the blessing for those close to God and the curse for 'the cowardly, the faithless' and such like. This is a typical description of the judgement and separation that we often associate with a picture of heaven. But before that part of the vision, there is the lyrical passage describing heaven as the moment of final healing: 'He will wipe away every tear from their eyes, and death shall be no more, neither shall there be mourning nor crying nor pain any more, for the former things have passed away' (Revelation 21.4).

I do not want to suggest the language of judgement can or should be abandoned for ever, but that people may find a more ready access to the vision of heaven by beginning with ideas of healing rather than of judgement. There is enormous scope for developing a picture of heaven as the place of final healing, for this includes righting wrongs, restoring the original blessing of creation and establishing lasting peace. Moreover, this example, like the first, draws on an experience that we know can begin now but that can never be perfected on this earth.

As you do this exercise you will be testing out new forms of expression for a key matter of belief on behalf of the Church. Once these expressions become familiar you will begin to incorporate them into your prayer life. Then the language which is already used in Advent and at funerals will be enriched for the ordinary worship of the Church.

So where does this leave us? We have been seeking a more ready access to the life of worship. As we enter into this worship, so we will recognize with greater clarity the majesty of God revealed throughout his kingdom. As we recognize more, so we have more involvement in that majestic life and are drawn further into creation's offering of praise. As we praise, so we are transformed and participate more in the abundant life of God.

> Accept us, Lord, as you have promised,
>   and we shall live.
> Renew us with your grace
>   that we may be transformed into the likeness
>   of your Son, our Saviour Jesus Christ. Amen.